The Last Steam Locomotive Engineer: R. A. Riddles, C.B.E.

Frontispiece: R. A. Riddles standing beside the *Duke of Gloucester* at Euston before his last journey on the footplate. *By kind permission of British Railways*

The Last Steam Locomotive Engineer: R. A. Riddles C.B.E.

by Colonel H. C. B. ROGERS, O.B.E.

London
GEORGE ALLEN & UNWIN LTD
RUSKIN HOUSE · MUSEUM STREET

First Published in 1970

ISBN 0 04 385053 7

PRINTED IN GREAT BRITAIN
in 11 on 12 pt. Plantin 110
BY UNWIN BROTHERS LIMITED
WOKING AND LONDON

ACKNOWLEDGEMENTS

In the writing of this book I am indebted chiefly to Robin Riddles himself, for he has spent many hours in answering my interminable questions and in writing voluminous notes, and has supplied me with many documents, papers, letters, and illustrations which span the whole of his railway career. But he would be insistent that the comments and opinions expressed are mine, except where his own views are apparent from the text.

I am most grateful to that outstanding locomotive engineer M. André Chapelon, *Ingénieur en Chef honoraire de la SNCF*, for allowing me to reproduce the letter in brilliant support of the steam locomotive which he contributed recently to *The Railway Gazette*. I must thank that journal for their courtesy in endorsing M. Chapelon's permission and Mr G. W. Carpenter of *The Railway Gazette* for his kindness in sending me his full translation of a letter which had to be slightly curtailed to fit the available space.

For many of the illustrations I am indebted to Mr J. Edgington of the London Midland Region, British Railways, who took so much trouble to find for me the finest photographs of the subjects which I sought. I am grateful, too, to Mr J. Spence, Assistant Curator of Historical Records, British Railways Board, for the time he placed at my disposal in searching for suitable photographs.

The character of the book owes something to that great and kindly man Sir George Turner, KCB, KBE, with his memories of the Ministry of Supply in the War and his humourous comments on men and events.

I owe a very great deal to the enthusiasm of my publisher, Philip Unwin, who has read each chapter on completion and has by his shrewd comments and questions, stimulated much of the argument that appears in these pages.

Finally I must mention my wife; for, if sloppy English is happily absent from the text, it is largely due to her devastating criticism.

CONTENTS

ILLUSTRATIONS

PROLOGUE

'The Great Western had the engines, the Midland had the carriages, and the North-Western had the road.' This is the assessment by Robert Arthur Riddles of the relative mechanical standing of the old railway companies at the time of the Grouping. Not that Riddles had any low opinion of London and North-Western engines: 'They were not thermally efficient; they burnt large quantities of coal; but you could hang 420 tons on to a *George* or a *Prince* and they went like the wind'.

The background to this biography, as well as the personality and humour of the great locomotive engineer who is the subject of it, are well conveyed in a speech that he made to a distinguished luncheon gathering in 1933, and it will serve as an appropriate introduction to the story of the last person to wear the mantle of George Stephenson. Riddles said:

'When considering the matter for this address, it was borne upon me that very few of my hearers would be locomotive men, and that in consequence I should have to speak in a language removed from the technical. I thought I might emulate the example of Professor Dodds, an eminent biochemist, who reduced the value of a dozen oysters to the equivalent of a piece of bread and butter, and in a somewhat similar way take the calorific value of the excellent lunch we have had to-day and illustrate to you how far the heat units we have consumed would run a train of the Royal Scot type. I had, however, I regret to say, to relinquish the idea, as I realized that a necessary ingredient in the working of a steam engine is water, and on looking round my worst fears are realized—there is not enough water available to take a train out of the station!

'My address, then, will be a short history of the past seventy years of the locomotive progress associated with the train now known as the "Royal Scot", because it was in 1862 that the first regular service between Euston and Scotland was instituted.

'The "Royal Scot" train from its beginning covers, to a large extent, the history of British railway express service. It has not always been known by its present name, but for seventy years without a break an express has left Euston for Scotland, and departed from Glasgow and Edinburgh for England, at the present departure time of 10 a.m.; and, as the 10 o'clock, this train celebrated her seventieth birthday on June 1, 1932.

'Railroads were very young when the first train ran between England and Scotland. The union of the two countries by rail was a very early objective of railway promoters and engineers, and as long ago as 1836 the great engineer Joseph Locke made a survey of the country north of Preston, with a view to taking the iron road through the Cumberland mountains to the Border at Carlisle, where it would join a line in course of promotion in Scotland.

'The Lancaster and Carlisle Railway was authorized in 1844 and opened for traffic two years later, carrying the line forward from Euston almost to the Scottish Border, whilst on February 15, 1848, the Caledonian Railway was opened throughout from Carlisle to Glasgow and Edinburgh. The first train to make the through journey between London and Glasgow left Euston on this same day at 10 a.m.

'The Lancaster and Carlisle Railway did not come under the control of the London & North Western Railway until 1859, but from that date until 1923 the Anglo-Scottish West Coast services were worked jointly by the London & North Western and Caledonian Railways.

'With the constitution of the London Midland and Scottish Railway in 1923 the famous West Coast Route became, in its entirety, a part of the great LMS system, and the 400 mile of track that separate London from Glasgow were placed under one management.

'Throughout its long and distinguished history the West Coast route to Scotland, over which the "Royal Scot" and her sister expresses travel, has been associated with a steady and rapid progress in locomotive design, and in the provision of increased travel comforts and amenities. Although the marked physical difficulties of the West Coast route have been met with a lavishness of engineering skill, modern demands for higher speeds and greater comfort exact from the locomotive the acme of performance in order that maximum efficiency of service may be obtained. The West Coast route includes two difficult sections—Shap Summit of over 900 feet in England and Beattock Summit of 1,014 feet in Scotland, both with sharp approaches. These grades impose as severe a test as can be found on any route in Great Britain upon the capabilities of locomotives, equipment and train crews maintaining express services over long distances.

'The following comparison of the regular scheduled times between London and Glasgow since the through service from Euston was inaugurated is interesting:

Year	*Time on Journey*	*Overall Speed*
1848	12 hrs. 10 mins.	32·9 mph
1862	11 hrs. 30 mins.	34·0 mph
1922	8 hrs. 15 mins.	48·7 mph
1932	7 hrs. 40 mins.	52·4 mph

It will be noted that there has been a progressive acceleration of the services, notwithstanding the enormous increase in the weight of passenger car equipment during these years.

'The various types of locomotive that have been used during the past seventy years make a very interesting study, and I propose to deal with five types of engine that have been or are being used for the "Royal Scot" train.

'The first type of engine regularly in use on the Scottish expresses, known as the Problem, or Lady of the Lake class, had large single driving wheels of 7 feet 6 inches diameter and cylinders of 16 inches diameter and 24 inches stroke. The steam pressure was originally 130 lbs., but was afterwards raised to 150 lbs. per square inch. The engine weighed approximately 30 tons. The Lady of the Lake class was designed and built by Ramsbottom at Crewe in 1859 for the Northern Division of the line and was at this time the smallest type of LNWR express engine in regular use; but engines only a few tons bigger were considered heavy. As a class they were very successful and Colburn, an early writer on locomotives, preferred the Ladies to McConnell's Bloomers which ran on the Southern Division.

'The next type was the Newton or Precedent class, the first of which was built in April 1866, and in this class there were three distinct divisions:

(*a*) The first 76 engines built by Ramsbottom before 1872.
(*b*) The second 20, built by Webb to the Ramsbottom design in 1872 and 1873.

(*c*) Webb's celebrated series of Precedents, turned out after 1873.

All the engines of this class, including the Precedents proper, were rebuilt to a greater or lesser degree, and in the Newton class only the wheels remained of the original engine. As compared with the single drivers of the Lady of the Lake class, these engines had an additional pair of driving wheels, with a pair of radial wheels leading. The engine weight was not much greater, being only 32 tons, but, owing to the coupled driving wheels, a much greater proportion was available for adhesion. This, together with a boiler pressure of 150 lbs. per square inch and larger cylinders, produced a more powerful engine. The Precedents made locomotive history and set a standard in practice which was not improved for many years.

'There is to-day still one of these engines in regular work, Number 50001 built in 1895, and it has run to date 1,994,230 miles. It is always a matter for regret when a veteran passes, but in a few months this engine will be withdrawn and cut up, and the Precedents will no longer be seen on our main lines.

'One of these engines, *Hardwicke*, a very famous old warrior, is being kept as a relic of the past and is now in comfortable quarters in the Paint Shop at Crewe. This famous flyer was prominent in the second of the great races between West and East Coast routes to the North. In the first race of 1888 the load consisted of four eight-wheeled carriages weighing about 80 tons, and the train was drawn by a Lady of the Lake to Crewe, and from Crewe to Carlisle by the equivalent of a Precedent. The second race of 1895 began with trains of up to fifteen coaches, but, as each route strove for increased speeds, the loads were reduced till, over the long and severe gradients north of Crewe, they were only equal to four and a half. The running was made by the 2–4–0 Precedent class, and pilot, or assistant, engines of the Lady of the Lake class were provided when the loads demanded it. *Hardwicke* made a record run, covering the 141½ miles from Crewe to Carlisle in 126 minutes, an average speed of 67·25 miles per hour. Another famous engine of this type was the *Charles Dickens*, which on September 12, 1891 had run one million miles in 9 years 219 days; a record equalled by no other engine in the world at that time and one which I believe is still unbeaten. *Charles Dickens* covered 2,345,107 miles before being taken out of stock.

'Between 1897 and 1903 Webb developed the compound locomotives for which his name is world-famous, and the history of which would provide a paper in itself. The driving wheels were not coupled and for this reason, and the valve arrangement adopted, they were notoriously bad starters. It is remarkable that Webb, who must have known of this defect, made no attempt to remedy it. Nevertheless, the Teutonic class compounds achieved considerable success, and on the last day of the 1895 race to the North one of them, *Adriatic*, ran from Euston to Crewe at an average speed of 64·3 miles per hour; an excellent performance.

'After Webb came George Whale who designed and built the Precursor class of simple expansion 4–4–0s with 6 feet 9 inches driving wheels and 19 inches diameter by 26 inches stroke cylinders. These were followed in 1905 by the 4–6–0 Experiment class, also simples, but with 6 feet 3 inches driving wheels for the more difficult road north of Crewe. It is interesting that the 60-ton Precursors were rostered to take maximum tare loads of 420 tons on the fastest services, which were in little or no degree inferior in speed to the best trains within very recent years.

'In 1910 Bowen Cooke built the George the Fifth class, which was similar to the Precursor but with the vital addition of superheating—thus beginning a new era in locomotive design on the West Coast route. The Prince of Wales class 4–6–0, also superheated, was introduced a year later.

'The increased weight of trains required still more powerful engines, and in 1910 tests were arranged with the Great Western Railway in which *Polar Star*, one of their famous Star class engines, was rostered to take the heaviest trains out of Euston to Crewe. So successful were these tests, and with such ease did *Polar Star* handle the load, that a new engine of the 4–6–0 type with four cylinders was designed for the London & North Western Railway. In January 1913 No. 2222 *Sir Gilbert Claughton* was turned out of Crewe Works, the first of 130 Claughtons, as they were subsequently known.

'These engines were a marked improvement on those already in service. They had four cylinders, 16 inches in diameter by 26 inches stroke, all driving on the leading coupled wheels. In

November 1913 an engine of this type, No. 1159 *Ralph Brocklebank*, put up a very good performance between Euston and Crewe hauling a train of twelve vehicles weighing 552 tons. The run of 158 miles was accomplished in 159 minutes, an average of 59·63 miles per hour including slacks and a stop at Rugby.

'I would like to mention here that the locomotive is generally talked of as a wasteful and inefficient machine; but whilst agreeing that its thermal efficiency is low, its utility and overall cheapness in hauling power is still supreme, even under present conditions. This lump of coal I have in my hand weighs just one ounce, and yet this small amount consumed in the firebox of a locomotive, such as I have just described, produces sufficient heat to haul one ton one mile.

'Following the amalgamation, traffic conditions called for even more powerful locomotives. Improvements and additions were made to the Claughtons, larger boilers were fitted to a number of them, and ten were given poppet valves. These measures resulted in a useful increase in power and economy; and then in 1927 the famous Royal Scot class of engines appeared. Fifty of these were ordered in one batch from the North British Locomotive Company, and in 1929 a further twenty were built in the Derby Works of the LMS. The Royal Scots have three cylinders of 18 inches diameter by 26 inches stroke and a boiler pressure of 250 lbs. per square inch. One of these engines, with a complete Royal Scot train, is at the moment completing a very successful tour of the United States and Canada. On September 9th this year a special train ran from Coventry to Euston hauled by the Royal Scot engine No. 6129 *Comet*, covering the 94 miles in 79 minutes one second, and attaining a maximum speed of 92 miles per hour at Castlethorpe. The average speed to the signal stop at Euston was 76·4 mph.

'In spite of the success of the Royal Scot class, the LMS are not sitting back, for modern conditions make ever increasing demands on locomotive power. Another engine has therefore been designed by Mr W. A. Stanier, our Chief Mechanical Engineer, to work the Scottish services. The first of this class was turned out recently, and it is capable not only of hauling greater loads than our Royal Scot engine but working costs will be considerably reduced due to its increased efficiency.

'These new engines have been specially designed to enable them to work through from London (Euston) to Glasgow and Edinburgh without requiring assistance on the heavy gradients, and the economies from this intensive use should amply justify their construction. They are of the 4–6–2 type with four cylinders of 16¼ inches diameter by 28 inches stroke, and the first has been named *The Princess Royal*. The fire grate area is much greater than that of the Royal Scot and this enables the engine to be longer in traffic without any clinkering taking place on the firebars, and is one of the features which permits long runs without the necessity of shed attention. Only two of these engines have as yet been built; the preliminary runs and tests have been very satisfactory, and the results so far obtained have been very promising.

'It has been my privilege to ride on this engine, and I was on the footplate when it made its first run from Euston to Glasgow hauling the "Royal Scot" train. We took a load in excess of the normal up both Shap and Beattock Summits without any assistance and arrived in Glasgow two minutes before time. The maximum speed attained was 76 miles per hour, but no attempt was made to set up any record and this speed does not indicate the capacity of the engine.

'In conclusion, I think the best illustration of the progress of locomotives on this particular "Royal Scot" train is the growth in tractive effort, or pulling power, of the five locomotives I have described to you. The first, the *Lady of the Lake* had a tractive effort of 8,423 lbs.; the *Precedent* 10,918 lbs.; the *Claughton* 23,683 lbs.; the *Royal Scot* 33,150 lbs.; the *Princess Royal* 40,300 lbs.

'I trust, gentlemen, that the few facts that I have been able to give have interested you and conveyed to you in some way the progress of locomotive building in this country.'

This sketch which Riddles gave of the history of the Anglo-Scottish services on the West Coast route is a very fair introduction to the problems of locomotive designers of the London & North Western, the London, Midland & Scottish, and British Railways; for it was this route that has presented them with the greatest challenge to their ability. In the end it broke Webb. Whale and Bowen Cooke succeeded at a cost, but help was requested from the Great Western. Hughes could not solve the problem, and Fowler's failure led to the Great Western being again asked for assistence.

Ultimately it was Great Western locomotive engineer, Sir William Stanier (but with the outstanding London & North Western assistance of R. A. Riddles, H. G. Ivatt, and the support of the Chief Draughtsmen H. Chambers and T. F. Coleman and the boiler expert J. L. Francis) who finally conquered the West Coast route. In later days Riddles, taking all that was best of London & North Western tradition, built engines that were designed by a driver, that were simple to maintain, and which ran into the magnificent sunset of British steam.

CHAPTER I

Early Days at Crewe

Robert Arthur Riddles joined the old London & North Western Railway as a premium apprentice at Crewe Locomotive Works in 1909. C. J. Bowen Cooke had just been appointed Chief Mechanical Engineer after the retirement and early death of George Whale. Bowen Cooke's appointment was a great disappointment to A. R. Trevithick, the Works Manager, who had been certain that he would be selected. It is said that when the news was brought to him in his office, he got up from his chair in silence and paced up and down the room in his characteristic manner, with his head thrust forward and his hands behind his back, whilst his secretary sat in embarrassment not daring to move. Suddenly Trevy, as he was called, threw his head back and said,

'Thank God! I shall see all my bloody enemies buried!'

'And', comments Riddles, 'he did'.

Shortly after this Trevithick was put in charge of Wolverton and W. W. H. Warneford took over as Works Manager. The latter took a great interest in Riddles and gave him much encouragement in the last year of his apprenticeship.

Crewe at this time was the most famous locomotive works in the country, perhaps in the world. The town itself owed its very existence to the railway, for when the main line of the Grand Junction was built there was not even a hamlet in the neighbourhood. A small station was established in 1837 at the spot where the turnpike road from Wheelock to Nantwich crossed the railway, four miles from Nantwich and six from Sandbach. Once the railway was established, there was considerable interchange of traffic here, for the 'Crewe Railway Coach' from Macclesfield through Congleton and Sandbach to Crewe ran twice a day in connection with the trains; whilst trains were also met by an omnibus to and from Nantwich and a coach to and from Whitchurch. The station was named after the neighbouring Crewe

Hall, the ancestral home of the Crewe family and the residence, when the railway arrived, of Hungerford, third Baron Crewe. His predecessor John, the second Baron, had been forced to allow the railway to cross his estates. In 1840 the little station became a junction when the Chester & Crewe Railway was opened. Two years later the Manchester & Birmingham Railway's line from Manchester joined the Grand Junction Railway at Crewe, which now became of major importance as a traffic centre.

Meanwhile, in 1840 the GJR had decided to move its locomotive works from Edge Hill to Crewe, and on June 20th the Board ordered the purchase of land for this purpose at Crewe junction. On July 1, 1840, Joseph Locke, the Railway's Engineer, was directed to prepare plans and drawings for the shops required to build and repair locomotives, carriages, and wagons. In 1841 Francis Trevithick, son of the famous Cornish engineer Richard, was, on Locke's recommendation, appointed Locomotive Superintendent.

In March 1843, the move of the Works from Edge Hill to Crewe was effected, and the disgusted Baron is said to have planted clumps of trees at all the points along the roads that crossed his estate towards the new establishment from which he would otherwise have seen this intrusion into his landscape.

In 1845 the first engine, *Columbine*, was completed at Crewe and it is pleasant to recall that this progenitor of a long and famous line of locomotives is still preserved in the Railway Museum at York. In 1846 the Grand Junction, London & Birmingham, and Manchester & Birmingham Railways were amalgamated, and the new concern was appropriately named the London & North Western Railway. But although Crewe was now the principal works, the locomotive shops of the other constituent companies were retained. At the Wolverton Works of the old London & Birmingham Railway were built the engines for what had become the Southern Division of the LNWR. These engines were designed by J. E. McConnell, Locomotive Superintendent of the Southern Division. The North Eastern Division, the old Manchester & Birmingham Railway, retained its Longsight Works in Manchester, at which John Ramsbottom was still responsible for its locomo-

Above: LNWR Precursor Class *Titan* at Brighton, 1909 on the 'Sunny South Express' during the LNWR/LBSCR exchange trials. (Riddles used to travel home by this train at the time.) *By kind permission of the British Railways Board*

Left: Apprentices at Crewe: R. A. Riddles is on the right. In the centre is J. L. Francis who designed the boiler of the first LMS Pacifics

Above: LNWR *Cornwall* at London Road Station, Manchester, about 1898 (Riddles drove this when it was used to haul Bowen Cooke's 'coupé') *By kind permission of the British Railways Board*

Below: LNWR *Coronation*: the five thousandth engine built at Crewe (Riddles remembers this photograph being taken in 1910). *By kind permission of British Railways*

Above: Prince of Wales Class *G. P. Neale*, built 1911 (*Edith Cavell* which Riddles drove in the General Strike was of the same class)

Below: Prince of Wales Class *Robert Southey* passing South Hampstead

By kind permission of British Railways

Above: LMS Claughton Class 4–6–0 No. 6014 passing South Hampstead

Below: LMS Royal Scot Class *Lady of the Lake* passing South Hampstead
By kind permission of British Railways

tives. At Crewe, Francis Trevithick produced the engines for the Northern Division, which comprised the old Grand Junction, Chester & Holyhead, and lines northward to Carlisle.

Sir Francis Head, in his *Stokers and Pokers* of 1849, describes the Erecting Shop at Crewe as it was in those days:

'The Erecting Shop at Crewe is a room 300 feet long by 100 feet broad, containing five sets of rails, upon three of which are erected the new engines and tenders—the other two being usually occupied by those under heavy repair. . . . In this magnificent building we saw in progress of erection twenty passenger-engines, also ten luggage-engines; and as this shop has . . . turned out a locomotive engine every Monday morning for very nearly a year, and is continuing to supply them at the same rate, we had before us in review locomotive engines in almost every stage of progress. . . . At the further end of the line of rails close to the north wall there appeared a long low tortuous mass of black iron-work, without superstructure or wheels, in which the form of an engine-bed in embryo could but very faintly be traced; a little nearer was a similar mass, in which the outline appeared, from some cause or other, to be more distinctly marked; nearer still the same outline appeared upon wheels: to the next there had been added a boiler and fire-box, without dome, steam-escape, or funnel-pipe; nearer still the locomotive engine in its naked state appeared, in point of form, complete—and workmen were here busily engaged in covering the boiler with a garment about half an inch thick of hair-felt, upon which others were affixing a covering of inch deal-plank, over which was to be tightly bound a tarpaulin, the whole to be secured by iron hoops. In the next case the dome of the engine was undergoing a similar toilette, excepting that, instead of a wooden upper garment, it was receiving one of copper. Lastly (it was on a Saturday that we chanced to visit the establishment) there stood at the head of this list of recruits a splendid brand-new locomotive engine, completely finished, painted bright green—the varnish was scarcely dry—and in every respect perfectly ready to be delivered over on Monday morning to run its gigantic course. . . . On one of the furthest rails, among a number of engines that were undergoing serious operations, we observed *The Colonel* [No. 188, a six-foot single built in 1847] which, by going off the rails at Newton Bridge, caused the death of General Baird.'

At Longsight, John Ramsbottom was Superintendent until he succeeded Francis Trevithick at Crewe in 1857. The North Eastern Division was in that year amalgamated with the Northern Division and construction of locomotives at Longsight ceased. In 1862 Wolverton Works too, stopped building engines, the construction and maintenance of which were now undertaken by Crewe for the whole of the LNWR. At the same time John Ramsbottom became the first LNWR Locomotive Superintendent. From 1865 onwards, the manufacture of all the Company's carriages was undertaken at Wolverton.

The original establishment at Crewe (now known as the 'Old Works') was too small for the much greater volume of work which now had to be undertaken, and between 1864 and 1880 it was enlarged by the construction of the 'Steel Works' and the 'Deviation Works'. In 1856 Sir Henry Bessemer had invented a new process of steel-making. After some difficulty he persuaded Ramsbottom to test some rails made of steel, with the result that the first Bessemer steel rails in the world were laid at Crewe Station on November 9, 1861. They were so successful that in 1864 the LNWR opened at Crewe the first Bessemer steel-making plant in the country. Associated with the steel plant were the forge and rolling mills which produced all the rails for the LNWR and the Western Division of the LMS until 1932. The Deviation Works were so-called because the Chester line had to be deviated to make room for their construction. They provided accommodation for a Joiners' Shop, a Saw Mill, and an Iron Foundry, of which the last later became the Millwrights' Shop. In 1876 new General Offices were opened to house the Chief Mechanical Engineer, the Works Manager with his staff, and associated departments. Other extensions and transfers of shops took place during the period that elapsed before the young Riddles, following in the steps of a great company of eminent locomotive engineers, arrived as an apprentice.

Of this arrival Riddles says:

'There was I, landed at Crewe, further away from home than I had ever been, working from 6 a.m. till 5.45 p.m., nine and three-quarter hours of actual work for the princely sum of 4 shillings per week; and this was followed by evening classes at the Mechanics Institution from 7 till 9 o'clock each evening except Saturday. Yet I enjoyed the work and often felt sorry that it was time to go home'.

He adds that although this may seem strange it was nevertheless true, and though the work was indeed heavy, he stood up to it very well. This enthusiasm and capacity for hard work were to last him throughout his career. As Riddles says:

'The Works were not very well managed in those days. Each charge hand had five engines under his control, and, as the boiler was repaired for each engine in the Erecting Shop, it was quite common for all five boilers to be under repair at the same time. Since some of these repairs took up to three weeks and more, the whole of the charge hand's gang might have little work to do for days on end. Shortages of spares were common, and often such items as $\frac{5}{8}$ inch nuts had to be taken from incoming engines to facilitate the repair of engines already in the shops. An assistant manager would sometimes come through the shop with a notebook, ask the foreman what he was short of, and, making a note of it, say he would see the storekeeper; but such visits were by no means frequent. From time to time obsolete locomotives were scrapped, and this procedure could be really laughable. Every one knew that certain classes were to be withdrawn, but I have known an engine of one of these stand on a pit for more than a fortnight awaiting the official condemnation—a chalk mark placed on the engine by the Manager himself as he hurried by on one of his infrequent visits. On one occasion we had been waiting so long that, having at last been blessed with the official chalk, my excited mate seized a big hammer and knocked off the steps—with the result that we had to use ladders to get on with the scrapping of the engine!'

Riddles enjoyed life, and, as he worked, he noted the various Crewe practices in manufacture and design. An advantage of the evening classes was that most of the lecturers were draughtsmen, so that problems could be discussed with them and answers obtained as to the object of certain aspects of design and any affect that they had had on maintenance. At that period, however, Riddles was not yet in a position to question or assess their affect on efficiency.

Riddles' first original piece of research related to locomotive chimneys. As he tells it:

'The old North Western chimneys were made of sheet steel, except for the top. I noticed that the centre part always had holes worn near the top, where a strip of steel 1½ inches by ¼ inch was riveted around the inside, and I set to work to find out why this ring had been put in. Without it no repairs would have been necessary because it was at this point that the steel plate corroded. The man who put the ring in did not know its purpose, nor did the Chief Draughtsman, and for a long time I could find no explanation. Then at last I came across an old man who told me that it was a water ring. This was interesting, but I could not think what on earth it could have to do with water. Eventually an old driver who had served under Ramsbottom provided the solution. He said that in Ramsbottom's day, when engines were really clean, the priming of an engine resulted in water being carried up the chimney and all over the boiler barrel covering, making an awful mess. The drivers found that by putting a worn piston ring inside the chimney the water was thrown back into the smokebox. The 'water ring' therefore became official. It was a small triumph for me that as a result of my investigations these rings were shortly abandoned.'

As Riddles passed through the shops his interest and keenness increased; he enjoyed it all and, probably because he was known as a hard and conscientious worker, he was given many opportunities to obtain practical experience. New work, that is erecting new locomotives, he found fascinating; but he learned more from repairing. In after life he realized how much he was indebted to the wisdom of men who had spent their lives in locomotive shops. There was, for instance, the old charge hand for new building who had supervised the erection of more than 1,000 locomotives. To him Riddles remarked one day that the managers must be very clever men.

'You get the job, Mr Riddles,' he replied, 'and you will find dozens to show you how to do it'.

Riddles comments: 'How true; but how difficult to determine which of the dozens is right; and in this, as I subsequently found, lies the lonely responsibility of decision.'

Its locomotive stud was something quite peculiar to the North Western; for the engines turned out by Crewe were not only the smallest that would do the job, but they were also the cheapest; and yet, with the exception of some of Webb's more temperamental compounds, they did a magnificent job—far better than those of some other lines which were more expensive and burnt less coal. But because of their cheap construction the North Western engines needed much maintenance, and of this Riddles says:

'The frame plates were too thin in section and had to be continually welded up; strengthening plates had to be put over the horn blocks; and with the heavy and cumbersome Joy's valve gear it was impossible to get constant lead in the valve opening in all positions of the reversing gear, and fractures of the motion were frequent. It was only when initial inspection was introduced that flaws were discovered and failures prevented. But whatever the merits or demerits of the stud, they would haul 420 tons out of Euston, sparks flying to high heaven, and many times during the periods of holiday traffic I have watched trains arrive at Crewe from London and heard the shed "turner" say to the driver, "Is she all right, Mate?" On getting the affirmative the tender would be coaled from a wagon alongside in Crewe Station, and off she would go to Liverpool, Manchester, Holyhead, or Carlisle. The Drawing Office, as I knew it "went cheap" and there was little in the way of failures to guide them. It was the good work of drivers, firemen, and shed staff, combined with North Western pride, that produced the results, despite defects in the tools which they were given.'

Riddles had not been long at Crewe before the exchange trials took place during which the LNWR Experiment class 4–6–0 *Worcestershire* ran Great Western trains from Paddington and a GWR Star class 4–6–0 came to haul trains over the West Coast route. The Great Western locomotive impressed Riddles:

'The trial with the *Polar Star* took place whilst I was at Crewe, and I saw this beautiful engine come into the station—the paint immaculate, the motion beautifully machined, and the footplate fittings polished. The engine not only *was* good, it *looked* good. Bowen Cooke had to do something and designs for the Claughton class were worked out. But there seemed to be the same old outlook and the same old questions were asked: "What parts can we use that we have patterns for? How shall we make the boiler, using as many of the existing press blocks as possible?" The result was a lost opportunity, for the boiler was much too small and inefficient. Even when a new and big boiler was fitted in later years it never matched up to the job, which depended as before on the skill of the driver and the hard work of the fireman for its achievement.'

Riddles did not, of course, have much contact with Bowen Cooke, but he impressed him as being rather pompous and wondered whether he had any great ability as an engineer. His designs were left to the Drawing Office which was still steeped in the traditions of Ramsbottom and Webb, and Riddles always found that they had difficulty in saying why things were done. Riddles adds:

'Bowen Cooke was something of a showman. At most stations, when he was on tour, he would hand the station master a telegram to send back to his office, at the same time making his identity known. On one occasion he called a foreman who was standing outside his erecting shop and said that he wanted him to send a message back to his office.

"Yes, Sir," said the foreman, and, taking out his book, wrote down the message in shorthand to Bowen Cooke's surprise.

"Do you write shorthand?" he asked.

"Yes, Sir."

"What your name?"

"Wood, Sir."

"Hmm." Within a week that man was made a chief foreman of the Erecting Shop. He turned out to be a good foreman; but that is how we are sometimes chosen!'

Riddles first footplate experience was in 1911, when all the 'premiums' and pupils were asked to volunteer for work during the strike. He was detailed to fire a *Jumbo* (i.e. a Precedent class 2–4–0) which had to fetch the District Engineer into Crewe. It was only a light engine, but he says that it 'rolled and rocketed about and I had great difficulty in getting my coal through the fire hole at all'. The District Engineer commented:

'You haven't been doing much of this.'

'No Sir.' I replied.

'I thought not,' he said.

As part of the training, if one were lucky, some weeks were spent on trial engines preparing them for the road and helping with the firing. Riddles enjoyed this and it was on these occasions that he learned unofficially to drive. On one such trial, on his twenty-first birthday, he persuaded the driver to go a few miles further along the line, where he dropped off to see a girl friend. She and her mother produced a bottle of champagne, of which he consumed a large quantity and staggered back to catch the engine on its return, accompanied by mother and daughter to see him off. Inspired by the occasion, the fireman had placed three fog warning detonators in front of the engine, so that his departure was signalled by a series of explosions which frightened the life out of mother and daughter.

Bowen Cooke used to travel round in his own special 'coupe', drawn by the famous old 'single' *Cornwall* with 8 feet 6 inch driving wheels. Riddles used to go on these trips sometimes, and on one occasion, when Bowen Cooke was not present, he drove this old engine. (The *Cornwall* is now preserved at the Transport Museum at Clapham Common.)

Riddles' main interest at Crewe was in the practical side of the work, and although he knew that he must get down to the technical study, he found it very irksome, save for the opportunities he had for discussing with the lecturers problems that he had encountered in the Works. However, not many weeks after he had first arrived at Crewe he read an article on electric traction in which it was stated that through electrification the capacity of a line could be increased by 30 per cent. This struck him so forcibly that he determined immediately to go in for electrical engineering and to direct his studies to that end. Pupils and 'premiums' were allowed to have a class on Friday afternoons, and at this they did practical electrical engineering, together with associated subjects. He obtained a fair measure of success, but, to his disappointment, he was moved to Rugby for further experience. Nevertheless, the result of that article, which so fired the imagination of young Riddles, can be seen to-day in the 25 kV 50 c/s electrification of the old London & North Western main line.

The outbreak of war in 1914 found Riddles in the Erecting Shop at Rugby, and he begged successfully to follow the example of many of his friends and join the Army. It was not long before Sapper Riddles of the Royal Engineers was in France.

CHAPTER II

After the First World War

Riddles spent most of the First World War in Field Companies of the Royal Engineers on the Western Front. Before the end of it he had been given a Commission and had been badly wounded. From a courteous Brigadier-General commanding a Guards Brigade he learned a lesson in leadership which he was to apply throughout his working life—that the more power one has, the easier it is to get results by asking rather than by ordering. (He was to find, however, somewhat sadly, that some subordinates would take advantage of such kindly guidance to over-emphasize their own contribution to these results.)

The War ended with Riddles out of a job. He wrote to Bowen Cooke, who replied that his old position in the Erecting Shop at Rugby was still open to him. He duly went back to Rugby, but this was a somewhat lowly occupation and as he was now married, he wanted a post with better attractions in pay and prospects. He could not put his studies in electrification to practical use because financial conditions after the War had halted any electrification plans. He had one offer of a job, but this entailed shift working with little likelihood of worthwhile promotion.

He was, then, when the 1919 strike occurred, a fully fledged fitter at Rugby. In those days a fitter had his own engine to strip and reassemble and the assistance of a mate. Riddles's mate, Middleditch, had been a Privileged Apprentice prior to the War, had enlisted at the outbreak, and had been demobilized as a Captain in the Oxfordshire and Buckinghamshire Light Infantry. When the strike brought the railway to a stop, the two of them decided to volunteer for driving or firing, and they were given the 'turn' for the Holyhead Irish Mail from Rugby. They took the engine out of the shed and were waiting for their signal, when they were told that the strike was over and that the regular crew had arrived. They were both then 'sent to Coventry', which they did not mind very much, but they wrote to H. P. M. Beames, the Works Manager, and asked to be transferred to Crewe. Beames agreed and posted them to the Millwrights' Shop, but they suffered some reduction in pay in consequence.

But Riddles and his mate had not yet heard the last of their action during the strike. The Unions after the War had become a lot stronger, and both of them had joined the Steam Engine Makers T4 Branch. They were in due course summoned before a Branch meeting to explain their conduct, and Riddles gives the following account of the incident:

'For some reason Middleditch did not go. I was in bed with a temperature, but got up and, having arrived at the address I had been given, was ushered into a kitchen where the Committee, except my accuser, was assembled. I then let fly and told them what I thought of them. I said that I had only just got back from the War, and that I was not in benefit, nor 'with Lloyd George' (as it was then called), that I had a wife and child, and that I had been in France whilst they had been striking for more pay and my mates were being killed through lack of ammunition. The meeting turned into a riot, the Committee assuring me of all they had done to get the men back to work! And then my accuser arrived. I just said that I did take an engine out of the shed during the strike, that I sat in it, that I would have driven it if needed, that neither he nor anybody else would stop me from providing for my wife and child, and that the Committee could do what the hell it liked. I then left. Eventually I received a letter from the District Secretary saying that although they understood, I must not "blackleg" in future.'

But Riddles was not left in such a subordinate position for long. On November 25, 1919 Beames placed him in charge of what might be termed one of the first pre-fabricated housing estates in the country. It was intended to overcome the shortage of houses in the town of Crewe and entailed the construction of some seventy dwellings. This task was to prove the first rung in the ladder which took him to the top of his profession. He had some qualification for it because after he had been wounded and made unfit for active service, he had been posted to a works company on Salisbury Plain. Here he had charge of a detachment of sappers, all tradesmen, and a mass of German prisoners, engaged on building aeroplane hangers, water supplies, quarters for men and women, etc.

Beames notified the departments concerned of Riddles's appointment in a memorandum which said:

'Mr R. A. Riddles has been appointed to take complete charge of the work of erection of these huts, in order to coordinate the various departments concerned. In consultation with the Estate Department he will be responsible for arranging, through me, all work in connection with the making of roads, drainage, and building of huts. From time to time he will confer with you regarding the sequence in which he wishes the work to proceed. Please give him all the assistance in your power to rush the job through in the shortest possible time.'

In his covering letter to Riddles, Beames exhorted him to have the work done as quickly as possible; he included a large number of instructions and suggestions as to how it should be done, and requested a weekly progress report. A motor lorry would be placed at his disposal for, amongst other things, obtaining ashes from the valley tip for making the roads. An amusing sequel to this was that the Borough Surveyor of Crewe asked if he could have half a dozen loads from this tip and was told that it was all required 'for our Mr Riddles'! In fact, this valley tip was, and is, a veritable mountain of ashes, amounting to many thousands of tons. Riddles endorsed this letter from Beames, 'My first job after the 1914–18 War'.

The way in which Riddles tackled the job impressed Beames, and before he had finished it he was given the additional task, to be undertaken at the same time, of building the new Erecting Shop, Steel Works. Beames's memorandum of September 23, 1920, referring to this read:

'With a view to expediting the building of this Shop and coordinating all Departments concerned, I have put Mr Riddles in charge. He will be seeing you from time to time with regard to the portion of the work for which you are responsible, and I wish you to give him every assistance with a view to the completion of the building in the shortest possible time.' (Beames seems to have favoured this particular rate of progress!) In a covering letter to Riddles, he wrote, 'Whilst supervising the work in connection with the above shop I wish you to keep in touch with the work on the huts'.

Riddles was now a marked man and soon found himself serving as a technical member on various investigation and economy committees. Beames had succeeded to the appointment of CME on the death of Bowen Cooke, and on December 15, 1920, the new Works Manager at Crewe, F. A. Lemon, instructed Riddles to deal with all building work foundations for machinery, etc. throughout the railway system, with responsibility to the CME (under whom at that time came all locomotive and associated buildings). A week later he was informed that he had been appointed 'Assistant to Works Manager'. It was a rapid rise from the defiant fitter of just over a year before.

In 1922 the London & North Western and the Lancashire & Yorkshire Railways were amalgamated. As the LNWR was by far the larger of the two it might almost have been considered to have absorbed the LYR, particularly as the former title was retained to designate the combined system. But from the locomotive point of view almost the opposite seemed to have happened. George Hughes, the LYR CME (an old Crewe man) was appointed to that post on the enlarged LNWR, and not Beames, who, having only become CME in 1920, was the junior of the two. In addition, Horwich, and not Crewe, became the principal locomotive works—a selection that may have rejoiced the leprechauns imported by Aspinall from Inchicore, but which could hardly have pleased the more solid English fairies of the Mercian shires.

It could not be said that the Lancashire & Yorkshire engines contributed much to the combined locomotive stock. Riddles categorized them as 'a mixed bag of indifferent types'. There were some useful goods engines and the 2–4–2 passenger tank engines had made a name for themselves; but for express passenger work the principal engines were the Aspinall Atlantics built at the turn of the century, which could run fast but could not pull, and the Hughes 4–6–0s which could pull but not run. Initially, each of the component companies continued to build its old designs, and each retained its old livery and numbers.

Hughes's first measure as CME of the combined undertaking was to institute a procedure which he called 'Coordination', and which entailed compiling a mass of statistics relating to the principal locomotives of the united companies. His most important constructive step was to decree that LNWR locomotives should be fitted with Belpaire boilers because of the small volume which the existing round-topped variety allowed for the disengagement of steam. But by the time that refitting started in 1923 the enlarged LNWR had been swallowed up by the LMS.

Another measure undertaken on the amalgamation of the two Companies was to transfer the responsibility for outside buildings to the District Engineers. This made Riddles redundant; but not for very long because he was soon placed in charge of a recording office at Crewe, known as the Progress Office. It had no executive powers, but it proved an excellent foundation for what was to become the Progress and Inspection Department.

The London Midland and Scottish Railway came into being on January 1, 1923. In addition to the LNWR and LYR, this enormous concern embraced the Caledonian, Furness, Glasgow & South Western, Highland, Midland, and North Staffordshire Railways. George Hughes became CME of the whole system with Sir Henry Fowler of the Midland as his Deputy. Beames remained as Mechanical Engineer responsible to Hughes for the area of the erstwhile LNWR; Pickersgill occupied a similar position for the Caledonian area; as did Whitelegg for the Glasgow & South Western and Hookham for the North Staffordshire. Administratively, motive power, following Midland but contrary to North Western practice, was removed from the CME's exclusive control, and the new Motive Power Department was responsible both to the CME and the Chief Operating Officer.

Rather strangely, having regard to the LNWR's traditional status as the 'Premier Line', Midland influence was predominant in the LMS, and it was Midland red which became the livery of both passenger engines and carriages. Crewe resisted as long as possible the crowning insult of painting North Western engines red, and managed to have large stocks of black paint to use up. This Midland predominance was due mainly to the powerful personality of Sir Guy Granet, the Midland Chairman, who became Chairman of the LMS.

From 1923 to 1925 a series of tests was carried out to compare the three-cylinder compound 4–4–0s of the Midland with passenger engines of the other amalgamated companies. The Compound proved the most efficient thermally and was immediately adopted as the standard type. But thermal efficiency is a doubtful standard by which to measure the suitability of an engine for its job. A truer standard is practical efficiency, or the ability to do competently the job required of it. By this standard Riddles had little use for the Compounds, for, whereas a George or a Prince could take 420 tons on the fastest schedules, a Compound could only manage 350. Double heading, therefore, became the rule, and whereas one Compound has a greater thermal efficiency than one George, the latter burnt considerably less coal than two Compounds.

'The North Western engines', comments Riddles, 'with their skilled drivers and firemen, did a thoroughly competent job in their day, in spite of their design. With hindsight and modern testing equipment it is easy to criticize and compare.' But the Midland regime liked Compounds and in addition to the 45 that they already possessed, no less than 195 were promptly built for the LMS. (Years later Riddles had the naughty satisfaction of having Midland Compounds painted London & North Western black.)

In 1925 Hughes retired and was succeeded by Fowler. With encouragement from Granet, 'Midlandization' now began in earnest. Not only the Compounds, but Midland 0–6–0 freight engines, both tender and tank, and the inside cylinder simple 4–4–0 general purpose passenger engines became the standard for the line.

At this juncture, the end of a locomotive era so far as the North Western was concerned, it may perhaps be appropriate to record the following list of LNWR engines (in the somewhat odd nomenclature of the old Company) which were still running on March 12, 1925:

6 ft. 6 in.	6 Coupled Express Passenger Engine (Claughton Class)	130
6 ft. 6 in.	4 Coupled Express Passenger Engine (George the Fifth Class)	90

6 ft. 6 in.	4 Coupled Express Passenger Engine (Precursor Class)	
	non-superheated	71
	superheated	57
6 ft. 0 in.	6 Coupled Express Passenger Engine (Experiment Class)	105
6 ft. 0 in.	6 Coupled Express Passenger Engine (Prince of Wales Class) (including Wembley Engine)[1]	246
7 ft. 0 in.	4 Coupled Compound Passenger Engine (Alfred the Great Class)	3
7 ft. 0 in.	4 Coupled Compound Passenger Engine (Diamond Jubilee Class)	1
7 ft. 0 in.	4 Coupled Express Passenger Engine (Renown Class)	70
6 ft. 0 in.	4 Coupled Side Tank Passenger Engine (4–4–2)	50
5 ft. 6 in.	6 Coupled Side Tank Engine (4–6–2)	47
5 ft. 0 in.	6 Coupled Side Tank Passenger Engine (0–6–2)	77
5 ft. 6 in.	4 Coupled Side Tank Passenger Engine (2–4–2)	155
4 ft. 6 in.	4 Coupled Side Tank Passenger Engine (2–4–0)	13
5 ft. 0 in.	6 Coupled Goods Engine (4–6–0)	170
4 ft. 3 in.	8 Coupled Goods Engine (0–8–0) (Class D)	61
4 ft. 3 in.	8 Coupled Goods Engine (0–8–0) (Class C.1) (Small Boiler)	34
4 ft. 3 in.	8 Coupled Goods Engine (0–8–0) (Class G) (Large Boiler)	82
4 ft. 3 in.	8 Coupled Goods Engine (0–8–0) (Class G2) (with Superheater)	274
4 ft. 3 in.	8 Coupled Compound Coal Engine (2–8–0) (Class F)	4
5 ft. 0 in.	6 Coupled Express Goods Engine (0–6–0)	308
4 ft. 3 in.	6 Coupled Side Tank Goods Engine (0–6–2) (Coal Side Tank)	289
4 ft. 3 in.	6 Coupled Saddle Tank Coal Engine (0–6–0)	44

[1] A new engine built by W. Beardmore & Co. in 1924, LMSR No. 5845, and named *Prince of Wales* whilst on show at the 1924 Wembley Exhibition.

4 ft. 3 in.	4 Coupled Shunting Engine (0–4–2) (Square Saddle Tank)	20
4 ft. 3 in.	6 Coupled Shunting Engine (0–6–0) (Special Tank Class)	234
4 ft. 3 in.	8 Coupled Side Tank Shunting Engine (0–8–2)	30
4 ft. 0 in.	4 Coupled Crane Engine (0–4–2T)	6
4 ft. 0 in.	4 Coupled Shunting Engine (0–4–0T)	11
6 ft. 6 in.	4 Coupled Express Passenger Engine (Precedent Class)	79
6 ft. 0 in.	4 Coupled Express Passenger Engine (Waterloo Class)	24
5 ft. 0 in.	6 Coupled Goods Engine (Special D.X.)	67
4 ft. 3 in.	6 Coupled Goods Engine (Coal Engine Class)	216
4 ft. 6 in.	4 Coupled Side Tank Passenger Engine (2–4–2)	70

(Note: The detailed wheel arrangements do not appear in the official descriptions, but have been added where it is considered the reader might be in some doubt.) In the latter days of the LNWR all except the last five classes were listed as 'Locomotive Engines which will be retained, and renewed when necessary'; whilst the last five were described as 'Locomotive Engines which will not be retained but will gradually disappear from stock'. Actually it did not work out quite like that, for examples of all the last five classes lasted considerably longer than some of the classes that were earmarked for retention. In Riddles' opinion:

'The grouping of railways did an immense amount of good for Crewe; for we had to organize. I was sent to Horwich for a month to study the initial inspection of locomotives coming in for repair. In this, the old Lancashire & Yorkshire Works, there was a very good initial inspection department, which laid down what was to be repaired or renewed and defined standards—removing all this work from the influence of the foreman and the shops. I came back full of enthusiasm; only to encounter a strong antagonism from Beames.'

In the end Riddles prevailed, but the story of his reorganization of Crewe Works belongs to the next chapter.

In 1926 there occurred the disastrous General Strike, and Riddles was given *Edith Cavell*, a Prince of Wales class engine built in 1915, to drive. He says:

'After a 30-hour standstill on the line, I took the first train from Crewe into Manchester, and did two round trips a day for the next two days. On the second day I set up a record from Manchester to Crewe; stopping at every station (thirteen of them) and doing the journey of thirty-one miles in under the hour—a feat which was noted by the Press. On the third day I was given a George the Fifth and I could not obtain anything like the acceleration and had difficulty in stopping the engine from slipping. But of course, once under way, it ran like a hare. On the fourth day I asked for *Edith* again, and was booked to run from Crewe to Carlisle with the Scotch Express!'

He had some difficulty in climbing Grayrigg, a longer pull than Shap though not so steep. He thought Shap would be more than difficult, particularly with a 'green' fireman, and so refused to start from Tebay until he had a full head of steam in the boiler. When they did get going he had to take a turn with the shovel himself, because the Princes and Experiments, with their long and level grates, were not the easiest to fire. As it was, he made a very fast ascent of Shap and arrived at Carlisle with no steam left at all.

The lesson of the extra adhesion given by additional coupled wheels was one which he never forgot and which was to influence considerably his own subsequent designs—culminating in a 2–10–0 which could, and did, run at 90 mph for British Railways.

Though many Chief Mechanical Engineers never drove a locomotive, Riddles maintains that the practical knowledge so acquired is an invaluable aid to anyone responsible for design. (The greatest compliment to his own driving ability came from Fred Bishop, the top link driver who was sent to America with the 'Coronation Scot'. Riddles overheard him say, 'If he comes on my engine I'll hand the corner over to him at any time'.)

The nameplate of *Edith Cavell* is now secured to the wall of the workshop that Riddles has built at his home.

(Note: Robin Riddles was lunching with me recently and we were discussing the relative merits of four and six-coupled locomotives. Leaving me to talk to Mrs Riddles, he went into the kitchen to help my wife with the next course. Presently in he came bearing a blancmange flanked by six half peaches, three on each side, and with a cork stuck upright at the top of one end. Putting it down in front of me, he announced triumphantly, 'Six-coupled!')

CHAPTER III

The Reorganization of Crewe Locomotive Works

On his return from Horwich in 1925 Riddles strove successfully in his progress Office to introduce some of the new ideas which Beames so heartily disliked. He was, in fact, in the right place at the right time, for the entire reorganization of Crewe Works at the (for those days) huge sum of £1 million had been authorized, and this was carried out during the years 1925–28.

At one time the pre-eminence of Crewe amongst the locomotive centres in Great Britain was never in doubt; so unquestioned, in fact, that a Crewe training was regarded as almost essential to those who aspired to high positions in the business of building locomotives either in railway establishments or in private firms. But as other railway works, such as those at Swindon, Doncaster, Horwich, Darlington and Derby came to the fore, so Crewe lost something of its former status. In addition, it began to suffer from the inadequacy of equipment and accommodation which had been built originally for a very much smaller railway and for smaller engines. The LMSR was faced with the alternatives of either scrapping all the existing shops and replacing them with new ones furnished with the latest equipment, or of reorganizing the whole plant as regards its methods, machinery, transportation and the distribution of labour, together with such reconstruction and rebuilding as was necessary to effect the reorganization. The first alternative was ruled out because it was both prohibitively expensive, and would also bring the whole Works to a complete halt. The second alternative was therefore adopted.

Successive extensions to Crewe Works had been carried out longitudinally to the west because there was no room available for expansion in width, i.e. to the north or to the south. The result was a rambling layout extending nearly two miles from one end to the other, and no less than nine erecting shops were spread along this length.

Riddles was placed in charge of the whole reorganization as Clerk of Works. It entailed completely altering the layout and building a new erecting shop of three-and-three-quarters acres. All the existing shops were changed round in the process, which would not have been too difficult had there been only new construction to consider, but which involved some complicated planning to avoid halting the repair and maintenance of locomotives. Riddles had a special gang of men, some 250 strong, who were engaged on a day-to-day basis, without any railway privileges. He could thus pay men off immediately if they became slack, and could interview and engage replacements. In time he had a really good team, and he found that by transferring the best of them from time to time to the permanent works staff, the effect on the others was as good as, or even better than, sacking a man who was useless. He was, in fact, learning a lesson in man management that giving credit when it was deserved was of greater importance than apportioning blame.

The whole of this reshaping has been fully described in 'Reorganization of Crewe Locomotive Works', published by *The Railway Engineer* in 1929 and compiled from a series of articles in that journal, for which much of the information was supplied by Riddles. The central feature of the organization was a new scheme for progressive locomotive repair which had been suggested by Beames and evolved by Riddles and which was put into operation in 1926 even before any of the reconstruction was ready. This was a belt system by which locomotives were moved gradually through the Erecting Shop until they emerged fully repaired. The effect was almost instantaneous, and when the system was in full swing the time for an engine under repair had been reduced from an average of 52 days to a maximum of 12 for the largest engines and 8 for small 0–6–0s, and some 100 fewer engines were under or awaiting repair at any one time. A considerable capital sum was thus saved. This belt system was the basis of all subsequent reorganizations of steam locomotive repair, and was adopted not only in the United Kingdom but throughout the world. Beames got the idea after a visit to America where he had seen the progressive manufacture of motor cars and thought such a system could be utilized for locomotive repairs. Actually the problem was entirely different, but Beames insisted on its being tried and, with everybody else helping, Riddles produced the final workable scheme. Ironically, it depended for its success on the initial examination (which was carried out in a matter of hours) of the entire locomotive before repair was undertaken—an examination to which Beames objected strongly, and yet without it his idea could never have been put into effect.

By supervising and organizing the appointment and work of inspectors, Riddles was able to show large savings in money and time. In his office he had histories prepared for each locomotive and so was able to have ready such things as new boilers and cylinders long before the engines that needed them were due for repair.

However, in spite of the considerable savings, Sir Josiah (later Lord) Stamp, President of the LMS Executive and Chairman of the Company was still not satisfied. He wanted to know the reason for the approximate £3 million annual cost of locomotive repairs; whether the engines suffered from recurring troubles or if the design of the locomotives was such as to entail heavy maintenance. He accordingly set up a committee to investigate the situation. Beames opposed this and when the committee arrived at Crewe he showed them literally hundreds of small documents relating to engine repairs which, he said, were impossible to separate. The response to this by the chairman of the committee was to ask permission from Beames to use his telephone

'For', he said, 'I must tell Sir Josiah we are not being successful.'

'Well', replied Beames, 'you had better see Riddles first; he is in charge and I am sure that he will tell you the same'. Riddles, however, did nothing of the sort, but produced his scheme, based on the inspection records which he had devised, and this so impressed the committee that he was ordered to go to London and explain it to the great man himself. 'A red letter day indeed', says Riddles. 'I had arrived!'

Although the main feature of the belt system was its application to the erecting shop, the same principle was extended to all processes of production and repair, with the object of ensuring that everything was done in the correct sequence; that work was moved to men, rather than the other way about; and that work undertaken was carried on continuously until completed, without any intermediate delays. The need for reorganizing had been recognized after the end of the First World War, and in 1921 a start was made in building a new erecting shop at the western end of the Works. However, work on this had ceased at an early stage owing to shortage of money, and it was not till March 1925 that reorganization really started.

It was decided that all operations connected with the erection of new and repaired locomotives should take place in one large modern shop, and that other buildings should be altered as necessary to meet the requirements of the new system. The nine erecting shops which existed when the scheme started had between them no less than 256 engine pits. For Riddles' new system only 72 were required—though a much larger output was secured. The enormous new erecting shop was 910 feet long and 194 feet wide. It had three bays in each of which were two belts, and each belt was intended to produce one completed engine each day (except Sunday). There was an additional centre road without pits in each bay which was used to convey material. On each belt there were twelve stages. The first two of these were devoted to stripping and were known as Stripping 1 and Stripping 2. The engines were brought into the erecting shop by an electrically operated traverser to Stripping 1. After initial stripping, during which wheels, cab, and boiler mountings were removed, the engine was moved by an electric crane to Stripping 2, where it lost its boiler. The engine frame was then lifted by crane to one of the four next positions on the belt, numbered as Stages 1, 2, 3, and 4. Here it remained on its stand for four days; the four work gangs concerned moving between these four stages and their four engines to do their own particular tasks. On the fifth day, the engine having got its boiler back, it was moved by crane to Stage 5, where it was placed on its intermediate and bogie wheels which had come back from the Wheel Shop. After completion of the tasks here, the engine was moved forward to Stage 6, where it became one of a series of six engines connected together by a steel cable which moved them forward stage by stage, until on the twelfth day, after Stage 10, the finished engine was pulled out of the shop. The first engine on this new system was turned out on May 5, 1927. Because all the component parts were processed in a similar manner, it was possible to have as many as five different classes of engine on a belt at the same time. No material was allowed to be left lying about, all stores and parts being brought to the appropriate stages two hours before they were wanted; dummy clocks placed by each stage showed the time for the next movement of engines on the belt concerned; schedules were issued for each class of engine, detailing the material that was to be stocked at each stage in anticipation of requirements; and before the winches were put into operation to move the engines, a loud buzzer was sounded as a warning signal. After leaving the shop the engine had a tender attached and was steamed. It was then sent on a trial trip; after which it was either taken to the paint shop or handed back to the Motive Power Department for service.

Control of the whole of these operations was vested in Riddles' Progress Office, where the records were kept and the daily programme of work arranged. The Progress Office was responsible for arranging the shopping of engines, their inspection, the manufacture of the parts required, the repairs to be undertaken, and for recording every phase of the work. Every day a meeting was held in the Progress Office under the chairmanship of one of its assistants and attended by foremen of the shops concerned to discuss the work on hand and the supply of all material. The minutes of these meetings were give a wide circulation and showed, amongst other things, the engines to be taken in for the various belts on the following day.

But the Progress Office was not only concerned with the engines whilst they were inside the Works. It kept in touch with the condition of all locomotives in service on the Western Division of the LMS. Standard times were fixed for each class of engine between heavy repairs. For the larger passenger engines, for instance, this was 12 months; whilst for goods engines it varied between 18 and 30 months. But whether an engine actually came in for overhaul when it was due, depended on its condition. Two months before an engine was due for shopping the running shed concerned entered its condition on a special form which it sent to the Mechanical Engineers Department. On receipt of the form an inspector was sent to examine the boiler, and following his report the Mechanical Engineers' Department decided whether the engine could continue in service beyond the prescribed period. If so, similar reports were compiled two months before the expiration of the extended period.

It will be of interest to follow the progress of one particular engine in accordance with the system described above. In 'Re-organization of Crewe Locomotive Works' the fortunes of a 4–6–0 engine of the LNWR Experiment class, No. 887 *Fortuna* are followed. On the shopping card this engine was given both its old LNWR number and its new LMS number, 5496. The card showed that the engine had completed 66,278 miles since its last heavy overhaul at Crewe and had been due for shopping in May 1927. It had been re-proposed for October 1, 1927 and agreed for shopping. On its 'Proposed for Shops' form of August 8, 1927, its frames were described as good and the tender as fair. The remarks on the form read: 'Truck wheels require changing, sharp flanges. Reversing gear in bad order. As boiler inspector gives this engine three months only I do not propose to do light repairs. The engine will continue to do local work when tubes have been changed'. The form was signed by the Motive Power Superintendent, Crewe. The detailed report on the boiler describes it on the whole as fairly good, and the Boiler Inspector gave as the 'Estimated time boiler will run before it requires shopping' as '3 to 4 months'. The Chief Boiler Inspector, Mechanical Engineer's Department, Crewe, thereupon instructed the shed staff to attend to necessary repairs, and the shopping of the engine was again postponed until January 7, 1928. On January 3rd it arrived at the Works and appeared in the minutes of the daily meeting at the Progress Office as to be taken on hand on January 9, 1928 on No. 1 Belt. In the Progress Office the Engine-Repair record cards showed that No. 887 had arrived 'On Shop' on March 27, 1925, and had been 'Off Shop' on May 6, 1925—that is a total of forty days. However, it was not 'Off Works' until May 24th. It had been in again between June 9 and 17, 1925, to have its buffer plate and main frames straightened. The vast improvement under the new system is shown by *Fortuna's* departure from the shop on January 21, 1928, twelve days after she had entered it. Two days later the engine was 'Off Works'. The examination report of January 23, 1928 on engine No. 5496/887 6A Class reads: 'I have examined the above engine which was turned out of South

Left: Royal Scot Class *The Royal Dragoon*

Above: Chambers, Riddles, Symes, Stanier, Beames and Lemon at Crewe, 1933, standing by the new LMS Pacific No. 6200 *The Princess Royal*

By kind permission of British Railways

Above: LMS Pacific Class *The Princess Royal* on a trial run

Below: LMS Pacific Class *Princess Elizabeth* on the Euston–Glasgow record run
In both illustrations Riddles can be seen in the cab
By kind permission of British Railways

Erecting Shop on January 21, 1928 after heavy repairs, and hereby certify that the repairs have been carried out in a thorough manner, and that the same is in good condition in every respect'.

On arrival of the engine at the Works the tender would have been removed and sent to the tender shop, where it would have also been repaired on the belt system, but not kept longer than four days. It had long been the policy of Crewe to have fewer tenders than engines owing to their quicker time of repair, and this tender would probably have been fitted to another engine when it emerged from the erecting shop. (This had some comic results in the earlier years of grouping, for Midland influence decreed that engine numbers should be borne, Midland fashion, on the tender sides. In due course, therefore, London & North Western engines could be seen running with tenders bearing the numbers of other engines, in addition, some black engines had red tenders and vice versa.)

Locomotive cabs, bunkers, tanks, and panels were built and repaired, also on the belt system, in the old Erecting Shop No. 9, which was now called the Erecting Shop North, and was parallel to the new Erecting Shop South.

In the Progress Office returns were made up from special boards on which were shown the daily movements of engines—the position of any engine being visible at a glance by a disc inscribed with its number. Another board showed the position of boilers.

The new boiler building department was on the south-east of the Works area in what is known as the Old Works and in the former Nos. 1, 2, 3, and 4 Erecting Shops. The belt system was also applied to boilers, and for building new boilers there were ten stages and seventeen berths. Under the new system a boiler was in the shop for only fifteen days as compared with the approximately thirty days it took with the old system. On leaving the belt, boilers were taken to the Mounting Shop where the tubes were fitted and the mountings were placed in position. The boilers were then tested both by steam and hydraulically.

The Tube Shop was in the old No. 6 Erecting Shop. The average time of completing repairs to an ordinary boiler tube was six minutes, as compared with three hours under the old system. The tubes passed through the shop in parallel lines; the fire tubes in one bay and the superheater tubes in another.

Beames, in the paper on the reorganization of Crewe Works which he presented at the Institution of Mechanical Engineers, summed up the results as:

(*a*) Reduction of transport costs.
(*b*) Reduction in the manufacturing costs of steel, locomotives, boilers and all components.
(*c*) Increased output of repairs and renewals, with a decrease in overtime and night shift working.
(*d*) Decrease in the time locomotives were out of traffic.
(*e*) Reduction in the quantity of portable tools and in labour costs.
(*f*) Lower supervision costs in the Erecting Shop.
(*g*) Decreased cost in electric current and gas.
(*h*) Greater ability to cope with the increased size of locomotives.

Apart from these direct benefits, the number of locomotives engaged in shunting within the Works area had been reduced by at least 20 per cent and the number of wagons conveying material had been reduced by 60 per cent. Fewer men were needed, but those employed earned higher wages. There was, too, the additional economy that all work flowed in one direction, from east to west.

The reorganization was the greatest event in the history of Crewe Works since the original move from Edge Hill, and a triumph of detailed planning and hard administrative work Riddles was now marked for higher promotion; but, nevertheless, Beames did him something less than justice in apportioning credit for the achievement. He circulated to all concerned an extract from a minute of the LMS Locomotive and Electrical Committee meeting of March 28, 1928, which read as follows:

'Mr Beames . . . also paid tribute to the staff who had assisted him and who had really made the economies possible, and in particular Messrs F. A. Lemon, Works Manager; J. E. V. Denning, Assistant Works Manager; J. Ryder, Steel Works Manager; F. M. Grover, Chief Draughtsman; and R. A. Riddles, who throughout had acted as Clerk of Works'.

But Riddles' achievement in the reorganization of Crewe Works was soon rewarded. On April 26, 1928, his promotion from

Assistant to Works Manager Crewe to be Assistant Works Superintendent Derby, was approved by the Board of the LMS.

Riddles' departure from Crewe was the occasion of some ceremony. At a dinner at the Crewe Conservative Club he was presented by his colleagues with a gold watch as a token of their esteem. Mr Ridgway, who presided, reminded the assembly that Riddles had at one time been apprenticed to him. In his reply Riddles said that had he been a parson he would have been inclined to preach a sermon, taking as his subject, 'When ignorance is bliss'. He had addressed them at the Progress Office on many occasions and talked to them about all sorts of policies and big things, which he was only just beginning to realize he knew nothing about. He thought that was why he was able to talk so well! He was going from Crewe, a place looked upon as one where great things had been done in the past few years—things of which they had not yet felt the full benefit. When in the future they did things equally well at Derby as at Crewe, they must realize at Crewe that it was because of the training received at Crewe. He could look on them as friends for life, and if ever he came to Crewe to ask for information—even if it was a dead secret—they would not mind telling him.

Many tributes were paid to Riddles in subsequent speeches, and the Works Manager, F. A. Lemon, drew particular attention to his outstanding success as a leader of men. At another ceremony he was presented by his own staff of the Progress Office with a gold guard and inscribed medallion. On June 23rd he left Crewe, and the head of the long list of signatures conveying best wishes was that of Hewitt Beames.

CHAPTER IV

From Derby to Crewe

At the time of Riddles' arrival at Derby, Midland ideas were still paramount in the locomotive world, but Midland theories on engine power had suffered a sharp reverse. After the Grouping the ex-Midland hierarchy had believed that the Midland practice of frequent and light express trains could be extended to the whole of the LMS and that the Midland Compound was the engine for the task. It was soon apparent that the North Western Anglo-Scottish traffic could not be made to fit this pattern, for the express trains that left Euston remained just as heavy as they had been under the LNW régime. The most powerful express engines that the LMS possessed were the 4-cylinder 4–6–0s of the old LNWR and LYR; but the North Western Claughtons, though fast, were under-boilered, and the Hughes L & Y engines, though more powerful, were slow. Something of a locomotive crisis faced the railway. It is not intended to repeat here a tale which has so often been told (and about which conflicting opinions are still held) of the events leading up to the crisis and how it was resolved. However, plans which the CME, Sir Henry Fowler, had for a compound Pacific were overruled. The Motive Power Department preferred a 4–6–0, for which the existing turntables would be long enough, and were able to point to the superiority which the Great Western Castle class engines had recently displayed over H. N. Gresley's LNER Pacifics. Accordingly the LMS, in September 1926, applied for the loan of one of these supremely efficient engines. No. 5000 *Launceston Castle* arrived in response to this request, and met all the traffic demands with such ease that at the end of 1926 the LMS placed an order with the North British Locomotive Company for 50 three-cylinder simple 4–6–0 engines. The first of these, known as the Royal Scot class, was turned out in August 1927, and the remainder were in service before the end of the year.

The publicity side of the LMS made the most of the new engine, characterized by its enormously fat boiler and diminutive chimney. The engines all carried names of either Regiments of the British Army or of famous early locomotives of the antecedent companies of the LMS. S. P. B. Mais was commissioned to write a booklet entitled *The Royal Scot and her Forty Nine Sister Engines* and the Company took occasion to produce a handsome volume, lavishly illustrated with plates both in colour and black and white, dealing with the history of its locomotives and those of its constituent companies.

From the first these new engines were a success, and at last the LMS had a stud of fast and powerful express passenger engines which could bear comparison with those of the other big companies It is true that, perhaps owing to the rapidity with which they were designed and produced, certain faults developed, resulting in heavy coal consumption, rough riding, and hot boxes, but modifications were produced to correct these and they did not interrupt the haulage of the fast and heavy expresses which once more, in the North Western tradition, were steaming in succession out of Euston with one engine at the head. It could not be said that Derby had had much to say in the design of the Royal Scots, but at least they had managed to insist on a Midland appearance. This did not suffice to save Fowler's prestige, which was somewhat considerably reduced.

Riddles' chief as Works Superintendent at Derby was H. G. Ivatt, a fellow London & North Western man who had arrived at Crewe as an apprentice about five years before Riddles. He had been Deputy to J. A. Hookham, Locomotive Superintendent of the North Staffordshire Railway, and had subsequently been appointed Special Assistant to Fowler. He had become Works Superintendent at Derby in succession to Symes, when the latter was appointed Principal Assistant to Fowler. When Ivatt was made Works Superintendent, however, Fowler gave him a smaller salary than Symes had been getting for the same job on the grounds that the latter was still available at Derby to give advice. But when in 1928 Symes left Derby to take up his new position as Principal Assistant to the Engineering Vice-President R. W. Reid, Ivatt still got the lower salary and Riddles, of course, got proportionally less.

Riddles learned much from Ivatt, who had a very tranquil disposition. He told Riddles to ease up as he was not at Crewe, 'And', says Riddles, 'brought me down to earth from the rush and bustle to which I had become accustomed. Indeed, at Crewe I had acquired the nicknames of "Blood out of a Stone" and "Ninety Minutes to the Hour"!'

At Derby Riddles set to work to apply the methods he had evolved at Crewe. Ivatt, in his own words, found him 'a wonderfully good assistant' and gave him a completely free hand. Between them, Ivatt and Riddles achieved a tremendous improvement in the organization of production and repair at Derby. They reduced the average number of locomotives in the Works from 140 to 62 or 64, and they had an arrangement that when the figure of those under or awaiting works attention was less than 4 per cent Ivatt would give Riddles a drink after 12 noon on a Saturday, and if it was over that figure Riddles would give him one; but Ivatt generally paid.

On December 10, 1928 F. A. Lemon, Works Manager at Crewe, wrote to Riddles saying:

'Position of Engine Power—W.E. 1.12.28

'On looking at the above return I feel bound to congratulate you on the figure you have achieved at Derby, and am proud to know that it is a Crewe man who has accomplished it, and sincerely hope that you will be able to maintain this low percentage, although I know it is a little lower than one can reasonably expect to keep it. However, be that as it may, I feel confident that your figure will be as low as anybody else can ever attain.'

The return to which Lemon referred said: 'The percentage of engines under and awaiting repairs is in one case down to 3·8 per cent of the total stock. This is at Derby where Mr Ivatt (late of Stoke) is Works Superintendent, and Mr Riddles (late of Crewe) is the Assistant Works Superintendent'. It is clear that Riddles had a free drink this week.

On one occasion whilst Riddles was at Derby it was necessary to erect a gantry crane to clear a site and place column foundations in preparation for a building to store boilers. The weather was bitterly cold and the job unpopular. Riddles had asked the foreman for more men and then for a junior foreman to take charge. The foreman selected was sent to see him but refused the job. Riddles promptly ordered him out of his office and told Ivatt that he would lose his Assistant for a fortnight. He then took on the job himself; a spectacle which naturally excited some curiosity. 'Men', says Riddles, 'started coming out of the shops to see what was going on, but when I told them they could lend a hand with a shovel they soon disappeared!'

Ivatt, in the meantime, had been pressing Fowler about the salary. The latter had a curious aversion to any kind of expenditure and it was not till January 31, 1930 that Ivatt was able to write to Riddles, 'I have pleasure in informing you that on my recommendation it has been agreed for your salary to be advanced from £575 to £625 as from the 1st instant'.

Another batch of twenty Royal Scots was built in 1930, but this was dealt with in Derby Works under the supervision of Ivatt and Riddles. The LMS now had seventy competent express passenger engines and train operating was recovering from the decadent shackles of Midland theory. In the meantime, at Crewe, Beames had become an enthusiast about Caprotti poppet valves and was fitting these to the Claughtons in an effort to improve them. Indeed, he had started to do this before ever Riddles had left Crewe, and had been pressing the latter to hurry up with the Caprotti Claughtons. Riddles maintains that Beames should have tried the Caprotti valves first on a smaller engine. As it was, the Claughtons being somewhat in the public eye, attention was drawn to the inevitable teething troubles experienced with this gear. Later, twenty Claughtons were given a much bigger boiler and half of these had the Caprotti valve gear. The improvement in their performance with the large boiler inspired a much more radical rebuild. Two of them were entirely reconstructed in 1930 with this boiler but with a three-cylinder chassis like the Royal Scots. These engines were so good that their performance was very little below Royal Scot standard, and twenty more completely new engines were built to the same design soon after Stanier's arrival and incorporating some of his ideas. Nominally they were Claughton rebuilds, but it is unlikely that they incorporated many, if any, parts of the engines they replaced. Nevertheless, it could be said that the London & North Western Claughtons, in a final form, were amongst the most successful of express passenger engines on the LMS. Initially, and almost inevitably, the rebuilds were called 'Baby Scots'—a title which was also inevitably frowned on by the management; and their official designation became Patriots, after the LNWR 1914–18 War memorial engine. (Claughton class engine *Croxteth* was one of the two engines rebuilt in 1930 and it was renamed *Patriot* in 1936 in place of the original Claughton engine of that name which was scrapped).

In October 1930 Sir Henry Fowler was removed from his position as CME and promoted to be Assistant to the Vice-President for Works. His place was filled temporarily by E. J. H. Lemon, who had been Carriage and Wagon Engineer, whilst search was made for a new CME. Beames was transferred to Derby as Deputy CME. In 1931 E. J. H. Lemon posted Riddles back to Crewe as Assistant Works Superintendent to F. A. Lemon. One of his first jobs, a rather depressing one, was to close down the comparatively new steel-making plant which, although it was small, was one of the most up-to-date and efficient in the country. It had been something of a triumph for Beames when he obtained authority to build this in 1925 as part of the reorganization of Crewe: and when the furnaces were in service the production of rails, bars, and sections cost far less than if they had been purchased. This upset the steel-making firms, and in due course they suggested an arrangement to Euston by which they would allow a large discount over a period of ten years if the furnaces at Crewe were shut down. This offer was accepted and Riddles had the painful job of closing the plant and discharging 500 men. He was temporarily in charge of the Works when the closure was to take place and shortly before the event he was told of an overheard conversation concerning a plot to wreck the plant on its last night. He promptly arranged that when the men booked in on the last day they would be given their pay and compensation, together with a day's holiday. So that if any plot had been hatched it was successfully foiled.

A lesson that Riddles learned from the closure of the steel plant was that any reorganization must be complete, and not partial. In his opinion Beames believed that if he got new furnaces the rolling mill, which was completely out of date, would have to be renewed to deal with the increased output from the steel plant, and that once the plant was in operation he would be able to get the authority to do this. Unfortunately the effect was precisely the opposite; for it was the additional capital expenditure that would be needed for the rolling mill which finally persuaded the LMS Board to accept the ten-year proposition from the steel firms. Had a new rolling mill been built, even though the furnaces had been shut down, Crewe could have bought steel ingots and billets and still made considerable savings.

The brickworks, at which had been made all the bricks for the new Erecting Shop from the clay dug out of the foundations, were also shut down. But in spite of these closures, there was a new and highly efficient Crewe; locomotive repairs were individually costed and progressed; all work was subject to a highly organized system of inspection; and the shops were operated with the most modern machinery and practice. In fact, the full benefits of the reorganization, which Riddles had mentioned on his departure to Derby, were now being experienced.

In January 1932 a new Chief Mechanical Engineer, W. A. Stanier, was appointed and E. J. H. Lemon became a Vice-President. But before considering the impact of this locomotive engineer from the Great Western and of the Swindon ideas that he brought to Crewe, it is worth while looking forward to the following year; for it was the 1933 tour of the Royal Scot class engine in the United States which was the culminating achievement of the pre-Stanier locomotive era. It is this tour that is referred to by Riddles in the Prologue, and which has the additional interest that it was followed by his own American tour with the 'Coronation Scot' a few years later.

Sir Josiah Stamp arranged for a complete Royal Scot train, with the addition of two LMS sleeping cars, to be sent to the Chicago Exhibition of 1933. The Royal Scot class engine selected had a number of modifications specially made, including new steel axle boxes, new wheel centres and tyres, a side bearing bogie, and additional frame cross stays. The axle boxes replaced the Midland type which, after a few years use, had been the main cause of rough riding.

Sir Josiah Stamp sent a message to the Exhibition addressed to the people of America. He said that the London Midland & Scottish Railway had sent this train 3,000 miles across the world because they were proud of it, having built it themselves, and because it was characteristically British and a worthy ambassador of the transportation service rendered by the LMS. The aim in submitting the train to the interest of a wider public was to get an endorsement of the numerous courteous complimentary opinions of the Royal Scot which they had had from transatlantic visitors who had travelled in it in Great Britain. He felt it singularly apposite that this year of 1933 was the fortieth anniversary of the World's Columbia Exposition held at Chicago in 1893 when the ancestor and constituent company of the LMS, the London & North Western Railway, had exhibited a train which was honoured by the highest awards that could have been bestowed. (The LNWR exhibit to which Stamp referred was a train consisting of Webb's three-cylinder 2–2–2–2 Greater Britain class locomotive, No. 3435 *Queen Empress*, with two passenger coaches.)

The universal interest taken in the Royal Scot train during its tour in America and Canada was extraordinary. At the Chicago Exhibition over 1½ million people visited the engine and train, and at all times during the open time of the Fair a long queue of people could be seen awaiting their turn to inspect it. In the thousands of miles that the Royal Scot ran on the American railways prior to the Exhibition, she was greeted at all the stations *en route* with an enthusiasm which the average inhabitant of Great Britain would have regarded as amazing; and this enthusiasm was reflected in the comments in the American Press. One paper remarked on the sumptuous and elegant fittings and the fact that the seats were across the train with only four passengers in the first class compartments and six in the third. It added, 'Yesterday evening, as the train steamed slowly along, every station had its quota of sightseers out to see the flyer pass through'. Another paper said that owing to the size of the crowd special railroad police had to be used to keep them moving steadily through the train, so that most people had no chance of a close look at the luxurious fittings, most of which were new to American travellers. It noted that the two sleeping cars were completely equipped with air conditioning apparatus whereby passengers in each compartment could command either hot or cold at a moments notice. The windows attracted much favourable comment and it was generally hoped that American lines might adopt something similar: they could be opened with one finger and by pressing a small lever they closed automatically.

Another paper commented that William Gilbertson, the driver, 'blew a whistle which was quite soprano, causing several low-brows to shout, "Peanuts!"' One prominent American paper said, 'Some deep vein of sentiment seems to have been touched by the visit of the train. Everybody of British birth or ancestry has welcomed it as a friend from home and heard its shrill whistle with reminiscent emotion.'

After the Exhibition the train continued on another extended tour of American and Canadian lines.

CHAPTER V

'Princess' Pacific

Riddles had not been long back at Crewe before the arrival of W. A. Stanier. 'And', he says, 'we started in on the 4–6–2 *The Princess Royal*—new ideas, new methods, an anxiety to please the new CME—all absorbing and exciting.' To most Crewe men, although they knew little about him, the advent of Stanier was more than welcome. The CME's department of the LMS had never settled down since its formation, and the successive CMEs, whatever their qualities, had little chance of forming an integrated department. Sir Guy Granet's policy of aggressive 'Midlandization' had antagonized London & North Western men and occasioned bitter jealousy and suspicion between those who had served the various constituent companies. Stanier they could regard as a neutral, with no affiliation with any of the companies absorbed by the LMS and therefore immune from suspicion of favouring any one of the old régimes at the expense of the others. Furthermore, he had been trained by the great Churchward and had served in a senior position in the CME's department of the Great Western, with its considerable reputation for locomotive design and performance. He was a man, in short, to whom those at Crewe felt they would be able to talk openly. Even Beames accepted Stanier gladly; for he had not been able to get on with either Fowler or Lemon, and the relief he felt at being responsible to a locomotive engineer compensated him somewhat for his disappointment at not being appointed himself.

The unfortunate death of R. W. Reid left a vacancy for an engineering Vice-President, and Ernest Lemon, who had supported Reid whole-heartedly, was appointed a Vice-President, but for commercial and operating departments. Lemon, on Fowler's disappearance (as mentioned in Chapter IV) had been made CME, rather to the dismay of Riddles and his colleagues, because he was by no means a locomotive engineer. Nevertheless, he had achieved fame as a production man during his time as Carriage and Wagon Engineer and both Sir Josiah Stamp and Reid thought highly of him. To fill the appointment of Vice-President for Engineering, Sir Harold Hartley was brought into the Company and given the additional appointment of Director of Research. But there still remained the problem as to how the vacant post of CME was to be filled. The selection of Stanier came as a surprise and there was much conjecture as to how the idea of bringing in an outsider had originated. It was only in 1968 that Riddles learned how it had happened. Lemon had discussed the problem with an outside business acquaintance, who made the revolutionary suggestion that the LMS should approach the Great Western and try to secure Stanier for the appointment. In due course Stanier was lunching with Lemon at the Athenaeum.

Stanier was above all an expert on machine tools, of which he had had great experience at Swindon, and he took a tremendous interest in machines. He would, in walking round the shops, stop by a machine and say, for instance, 'It is not going at its proper speed', or, 'You must try [such and such] a cutting tool', or, 'That job would be better dealt with on [another type of] machine'. When met with the excuse that there was no such tool or machine in the Crewe shops, he would reply, 'Get it'. Stanier would always favour a machine tool renewal programme, and in the end, Riddles says, the LMS had the latest and best machines in the country, either in railway or privately owned shops.

To get everybody working together, Stanier had to get on as quickly as he could with the new designs—designs which should obviously be not North Western nor Midland, but LMS. 'And of course', says Riddles, 'as we all wanted to show our new master how good we all were, he had the utmost cooperation from everybody'. A wind of change blew through Crewe, Derby, Horwich, and St Rollox. Many Swindon practices were of course adopted both in design and workshop; practices which were much more elaborate and expensive than had ever been used at Crewe. Stanier, indeed, had been rather horrified at the traditional Crewe way of doing things on the cheap and producing engine fittings 'as cast', practices which went back to the days of Ramsbottom. But having gone out of their way to select Stanier from another railway, the LMS authorities could hardly object to his demands for the equipment he needed to introduce the standards for which he had been selected. In the meantime the plans for the 4–6–2 were going ahead. Chambers was the Chief Draughtsman at the time and it is conceivable that for some reason he omitted to draw Stanier's attention to particular requirements of LMS conditions; for there were certainly teething troubles which could have been avoided had Stanier appreciated those conditions. Nevertheless the new Pacific was a success and, indeed, far superior to any express locomotive that had previously run on the lines composing the LMS.

The background to this big new engine lay in the conditions of the times. Trade depression and strenuous competition from road transport were affecting railway revenues seriously, and many different schemes were being studied for retaining the existing traffic on the railways and for tempting back from the roads some of that which had been lost. For passenger traffic the LMS had decided on a programme of more trains, faster trains, and more attractive trains; and the question was being asked whether, as a commercial proposition, it would be possible to run through from Euston to Glasgow, a distance of more than 400 miles, without an intermediate stop. Before 1933 no locomotive on the LMS, not even a Royal Scot, could do such a journey as a regular performance.

'Stanier', remarks Riddles, 'faced the task of providing one'. He no doubt had the ghost of *The Great Bear* before him, and that experience and the success of Gresley's Pacifics persuaded him to set about the task of designing a large Pacific type engine. The result was *The Princess Royal* with four cylinders, 250 lbs. per square inch pressure, and a tractive effort of 40,300 lbs. This locomotive and one other similar to it were built at Crewe in 1933 when Riddles was Assistant Works Superintendent. They worked literally day and night in the shops to get the prototype ready by the date that had been fixed for inspection by the Directors at Euston. The boiler was far the biggest ever yet built at Crewe and presented a continual problem, even to the clothing. The old North Western boiler covering, to which Crewe was accustomed, was merely a poor quality felt, which was whitewashed on one side and which after a short time was completely scorched away between the lagging bands. (This very poor covering, however, gave Riddles the idea, which he used on his 'Austerity' engines, that there was in fact no need to lag the boiler at all, provided that the space between the boiler and lagging plates was airtight. He thus saved much time and money without a great loss of heat. 'Still air', he says, 'is a fine insulator.') But the lagging for Stanier's Pacific was a very different affair and was derived from Great Western practice. It was a kind of loose asbestos covering firebox and barrel; but it arrived in this loose state, and the problem was to get it on. Riddles says that he went down to the boiler testing shop late one night to find them all in despair. They had been told to put the covering on whilst the boiler was hot under test, but it would not stick. He was at a loss at first to know what on earth to do. Suddenly he remembered an occasion when he had been building those quarters on Salisbury Plain. Some of them were stucco finished and he had been intrigued to see his German prisoners standing with buckets of stone and gravel and throwing handfuls with such force that they stuck. Was this the answer to the problem? He told one of the men to bring him a bucket of the stuff, and he says:

'I took a handful and threw it at the barrel, and to my delight it stuck there. By 2.30 in the morning the barrel was beautifully and evenly covered. But I had forgotten all about my wife, who had insisted on coming with me to the Works and was sitting in the car outside on the road. Fortunately she was peacefully asleep.'

Work continued night and day on the 4–6–2 and the great day for its journey to Euston arrived all too soon. There was no time for any preliminary trial, for, hard as they had worked, they could not get the engine ready to leave the Works until the day before the inspection. At 5 a.m., therefore, the Pacific left the Works, without any previous trial in steam, to run the 158 miles to Euston 'light engine' in the gentle time of ten hours—none too long a time for an untried engine which was the first of a new class. It had been arranged that Riddles should ride on the footplate as far as Rugby where he would hand over to the Works Superintendent, F. A. Lemon. Buckets of oil were carried on the footplate and frequent stops were made, 'just in case', whilst examinations were carried out and much oil was poured on. The news of the new engine had got around and even at that early hour they were accorded something of a triumph. Every station on the route had heard of the engine's journey and it appeared to Riddles as if the whole railway had turned out to cheer them as they went slowly past.

From Rugby Riddles returned to Crewe, and there he saw at the top of the station the materials van 'with lots of pieces in it'. This turned out to be the special tackle for drawing the crosshead of *The Princess Royal* and he wondered what on earth had gone wrong. He soon found out that the crosshead had overheated and the metal run out twelve miles beyond Rugby. It was a design fault which was put right eventually, but the engine had to go back to Rugby to have the slide block re-metalled—a task which entailed a somewhat hectic night for all concerned. Nevertheless the engine was on view at Euston the following day. I can remember my own intense interest in the newspaper photographs, but I little knew of the drama behind them.

This first LMS Pacific was one of the loveliest engines to run on any railway in the world. As one would have expected, she had very much of a Great Western look, but the lines were far more graceful than those of the Swindon products. A minor blemish was the Midland red livery, which did not seem to suit her, and she would have looked far better in the traditional Crewe lined out black livery. Locomotive liveries are matters about which some people feel very strongly, and we shall be returning to the subject later when Riddles had to deal with it in respect of his own locomotives for British Railways. But a nicely lined out black takes a lot of beating, whether on a locomotive or a motor car.

On July 1, 1933, shortly after *The Princess Royal* was turned out at Crewe, Riddles was transferred to London as Stanier's assistant to take the place of Symes who had been promoted to Stores Superintendent. He says, 'I wasn't asked to go; I was told to go.' The information was conveyed to him by Beames, and he protested mildly because the moves to Derby and back had been expensive. Beames asked him what salary he would like as he was to see the Chief (as he called him) the next day. However, Riddles knew that whatever salary he was going to get must have already been approved by the Board, so that there was nothing Beames could do to change it; but he did find out that Beames hoped to go to London as Deputy CME and that Riddles would then assist him. Riddles says that his interview with Stanier started off with a discussion about *The Princess Royal* and future plans. 'This

Above: LMS *Princess Margaret Rose* on the 'Royal Scot' in the Lune Valley

Below: Princess Margaret Rose on the Liverpool–Euston express passing King's Langley

By kind permission of British Railways

Above: Jubilee Class 4–6–0 *India*. *Below:* LMS Pacific Class No. 45653 in B.R. days

By kind permission of British Railways

continued for some time and I was wondering when he was coming to the point of the interview. Suddenly Stanier said, "Oh, by the way, I want you up here on Tuesday." I meekly said, "Yes, Sir." As I went out of the door he said, "The Directors have agreed to double your salary." It was a good thing I was holding on to the door.'

Riddles says that it was 'not till Stanier came with shades of Churchward that the LMS really began to take shape. But even he had to go through a period of trial and error. His greatest success, if one could select any one thing, was the very efficient boiler for which he was responsible. But Stanier himself gave credit for the detail design of this to J. L. Francis, a draughtsman at Crewe, and never heard of perhaps outside Crewe. He started his apprenticeship in the same month and year as I did.'

It was after Riddles' move to London and whilst Stanier was away that a run to Crewe and back behind *The Princess Royal* was arranged for the Press. Ernest Lemon rode on the footplate whilst Riddles leaned out of a carriage window. Some ten miles south of Stafford the train came to a stand. Riddles jumped on to the track and went up to the engine, to find the left hand driving box aflame. The driver had sensed it was running hot and got forward to it by climbing through the cab window and creeping along (though how he managed it puzzled Riddles). He then poured oil on it from the top, and this became so hot that it burst into flame. Lemon asked Riddles what they were to do. It was a nasty problem, for they had all the Press on board and it would take at least an hour to get another engine coupled up. On the other hand if they ran the engine as it was, anything might happen. Riddles decided to risk running the train on at a reduced speed and gave the necessary instructions. Luck was with them, and they arrived at Crewe forty-five minutes late, but at least they had arrived, and the newspaper correspondents were very good about it. The axle, however, was so badly scored that it had to be scrapped. The only engine available for the return journey was a Scot which was ready for the Works. Riddles says:

'A *Daily Telegraph* correspondent asked me if he could ride the engine. "Certainly", I replied, trying to pour oil on the troubled waters. Then I said to the driver, "Go like hell; you have a clear road". And he did. The expression on the face of *The Daily*

Telegraph correspondent on our arrival at Euston was far from happy. "I've no guts left", he said; and the poor chap had indeed suffered an appallingly rough ride.'

The boiler of the new Pacifics required some modification. Stanier had insisted on the Great Western ideas of limited superheat, and it soon became clear that this was insufficient for LMS conditions. Early in 1935, therefore, the two Pacifics, No. 6200 *The Princess Royal* and No. 6201 *Princess Elizabeth* were fitted with boilers having 32 instead of the previous 16 superheater flues. As a result the already excellent performance was considerably improved. In June 1935 a test run was made from Crewe to Euston by No. 6200 *The Princess Royal* with Riddles on the footplate. The train concerned was the up Liverpool express booked to cover the 152·7 miles from Crewe to Willesden in 142 minutes. But with a load specially increased to 453 tons the run was made in 129 minutes 33 seconds at 70·7 mph. This was one of a carefully planned series of build-up tests, carried out on various routes with different loads to see whether the new locomotives would fulfil the job for which they had been designed.

The culmination to which these test runs were working was to run a train between Euston and Glasgow, a distance of 401½ miles, in six hours. This entailed much reorganization of the traffic (the timings of some 200 trains had to be adjusted for the down journey alone) and much careful preparation of the engine, No. 6201 *Princess Elizabeth*. The run was arranged for Monday November 16, 1936, and all Sunday was taken up in getting the locomotive ready.

Riddles now takes up the tale of the dramatic performance which followed:

'In the morning at Willesden I watched the coaling-up with nine tons of hand-picked coal. No. 6201 was fitted with a speedometer specially for the occasion and was gone over with the proverbial tooth-comb. Similar treatment was given to No. 6200 *The Princess Royal*, which was being prepared as a stand-by engine. Calculation was made of the best possible train-loading consistent with the high average speed demanded. I was to ride on the footplate and had had a continuous diagram made, on two small rollers, covering the whole of the journey. This diagram showed gradients, speed restrictions (amounting to fifty, all of which had to be strictly observed) and a theoretical curve of speeds which would be needed to maintain the six-hour schedule. This apparatus was suspended from my neck in a special case, so that by turning a screw I could wind the diagram from one roller to another as the journey progressed.

'Before leaving Willesden I had impressed on the Mechanical Inspector that he must make sure that all steam pipe joints were tight in the smokebox. Judge my consternation when at 5.15 p.m. he telephoned me to say that the left-hand main steam pipe joint had failed! This was a special stainless steel coned joint and was not available locally. It was too late to transfer all the special test fittings to No. 6200. I telephoned R. C. Bond, Assistant Works Superintendent Crewe, at his home and asked him to get a spare fitting from the Works and send it to me by the driver of the 6.46 p.m., which was the last that day from Crewe. (The next one did not leave till after midnight.) I was extremely anxious, in fact, as to whether Bond would be able to get the part in time, because the Works would be closed and in darkness, and the store was an immense place containing thousands of spare parts. However, Bond went straight to the house of a retired storekeeper called Frogatt who knew the place intimately and where everything was kept. Frogatt was fortunately in and led Bond straight to the right rack, where they found the joint; and Bond was just in time to hand it to the driver of the 6.46. I met the train at Euston about 10 p.m., rushed the joint out to Willesden, and by 2.30 a.m. the job was done and the fire lit.

'At 9.50 a.m. we were given the "right-away" from Euston. The run which followed was remarkable, as extracts from the official record show. With seven vehicles weighing 225 tons tare we covered the 401·4 miles between Euston and Glasgow in 353 minutes 38 seconds non-stop, at an average speed of 68·1 mph. The maximum speed reached was 95·7 mph and 83 mph was sustained for 12 miles on practically level track. The ascent from Carnforth to Shap summit was a record—31·4 miles to an altitude of 916 feet at an average speed of 70·5 mph; and the ten miles of Beattock incline were covered in 9½ minutes without the speed dropping below 56 mph. Our arrival at Glasgow 6½ minutes early was a great thrill, and to my relief the Inspector, on going round the engine, pronounced everything to be in order and cold.

'We had tea at the Central Hotel in Glasgow, and the train passengers, LMS officials, and the Press were most enthusiastic over their day's experience. After tea E. J. H. Lemon, a Vice-President, got hold of me and suggested that we ought to try and run even faster on the return to London the next day. But I was opposed to trying higher speeds and suggested adding an extra coach. Lemon agreed to this.

'Later in the day we all sat down to dinner with the Scottish Directors—chief officals of the Company, Press representatives, driver and fireman—and all seemed set for a happy celebration. Half way through dinner I was tapped on the shoulder and told I was wanted on the telephone. A voice the other end said, "I am sorry to tell you that my examining fitter has found all the metal out of the left hand slide block". This was an awful blow; what on earth was I to do? We were due to leave again next day at 1.15 p.m. and I was told that they had not even a Scot in good order. I said, "Get the engine to St Rollox; start stripping down; I will be there as soon as I can". An hour later, I having been sitting without saying a word to the by now happy company, Lemon looked at me and said, "You look tired; you had better get to bed; a big day to-morrow".

'"Yes, Sir," I said. "I would like to"; and made my escape. But what a job faced me at St Rollox! We had already experienced a lot of trouble with these crossheads, and I had arranged some months before for a centre line to be marked right round them to avoid taking out the pistons each time. This precaution saved the day; for even with this advantage it was not till 5.30 a.m. that we were coupled up again, and then had to be hauled off to the shed for firing up and preparation.

'As we were about to leave Glasgow Central on the return journey, one of our publicity men came up and asked me to warn the driver that the film people would have very brilliant lights on the platform at Euston. I was wondering if we would ever reach Beattock with a newly metalled slide block! But just an hour later we swept over Beattock summit at 66 mph and, despite bad weather, went on to reach Euston 16 minutes inside the six hours, an average speed of exactly 70 mph. In the two days we had run an aggregate distance of over 800 miles at a mean speed of 69 mph, which was a world's record for steam traction. When we got to Euston, Lemon came up to me and asked, "Riddles, why did you lose a minute to Beattock?" There was no appropriate answer!'

It was an amazing performance; but few at the time realized how close failure had been. That it succeeded was due entirely to the drive, determination, and tireless energy displayed by Riddles. The strain must have been tremendous. He had had little sleep on the night before the run, practically none at Glasgow, and he had travelled 800 miles on the footplate taking constant records, and without any relaxation from the tension and anxiety until the train finally rolled to a stop in Euston. And this was no 'stunt' run. It was an attempt by the LMS authorities to assess the practicability of a very high speed service between London and Glasgow.

It was clear that the high speed service envisaged could be operated, but it was also clear that much would have to be done to the track. The cost of the fifty speed restrictions in time and coal, for instance, was worked out and found to be considerable.

The LMS Civil Engineers now took matters in hand. In the Engineer's Office was a small specialized staff called the Hallade Section. They made runs each year over all the LMS main lines with an instrument known as the Hallade Track Recorder. The charts produced by this machine showed in detail any bad-running lengths of track and the faults which caused them, e.g. poor alignment, irregular super-elevation, indifferent packing with consequent low joints. Before this time most curves were laid in as circular, with half the required cant being developed on the straight. This system, however, frequently produced an undesirable roll, and by 1933 a proper transition curve had been adopted, in which the radius was attained by 'straight line progression'. With this method, as the true radius of the curve is reached, so is the cant applied at the same rate. If such a curve is entered at the designed speed, there is no excessive thrust either outwards or inwards. Before a really high speed service could be contemplated, the engineers were faced with the problem of redesigning these curves, originally intended for speeds of 60 to 70 mph, to allow speeds of 75 to 90 mph. The reconstruction of the track was a remarkable feat because the engineers only had six months in which to do it before the fast services were to start, which the run of the *Princess Elizabeth* had heralded. The tasks to be done included the complete redesign of junctions, cutting back station platforms so that curves could be trued to a better alignment, removing load-gauge restrictions, dealing with subsidences under the line, and even training Hallade draughtsmen in curve design.

At Polesworth, 3½ miles south of Tamworth, there was an example of a serious mining subsidence. A stretch of track about 1¼ miles long was affected and over this speed was restricted to 45 mph. The surrounding terrain was virtually a lake and the track had been lifted from time to time on ashes, to such a degree that the tops of the telegraph poles were at the level of the track, and a platelayer's cabin had completely disappeared. The LMS bought the coal seams affecting the track, and the work of ballasting the track and adjusting the curve was put in hand. 10,000 tons of ballast were needed, but within three months of starting work the speed restriction was raised from 45 to 80 mph.

Of the many junctions which were dealt with perhaps that at Stafford was the most notable. Here the Birmingham lines joined the main lines and there was a speed limit in all directions at the junction. An entirely new layout was designed, incorporating a new type of junction called 'two-level'. Speed through the junction over the Birmingham lines was still restricted to 30 mph, but over the main lines it was raised to 55 mph. A total of 1,820 yards of new points and crossings were installed during the reconstruction.

Normally the introduction of speeds up to 90 mph would have resulted in a further crop of speed restrictions, and much careful planning by the engineer's office was necessary to prevent this. Indeed no less than twenty-four potential restrictions were successfully avoided. In addition ten of the worst existing restrictions were materially eased and six others were eliminated.

The eventual dramatic prelude to the new service is told in a later chapter.

CHAPTER VI

The Stanier Era

Though the twelve Pacifics had been wanted badly for the heavy long distance express trains, there was a sore need for replenishing the whole LMS locomotive stock when Stanier took over the reins as CME. Midland policy had proved a complete failure; and approximately a decade after the Grouping the bulk of LMS passenger and freight traffic was being worked by locomotives which were too light for the job or which were inherited from the constituent companies and were rapidly wearing out. They comprised a multitude of different types of very largely indifferent design.

Stanier, as we have seen, obtained authority for the construction of twenty more Patriots for the medium express trains, so that with the Royal Scots there was now a capable stud of 92 three-cylinder 4–6–0 express engines. Of other useful locomotives there were 235 mixed traffic 2–6–0s, designed and built at Horwich, and 75 2–6–4 tank engines. (These latter were the best of the designs for which Fowler was responsible, whereas the 2–6–2 tank engines, built at the same time, were about the worst.) Easily the best heavy goods engines were the ex-LNWR G2 0–8–0s (a Derby copy of these intended as a standard design was a failure). The standard engines for light goods work were the Midland type Class 4 0–6–0s.

To meet the immediate needs of the railway six new designs were prepared with a standard range of Swindon-type boilers. Stanier had decided on these because although the parallel boilers of the Royal Scots and Patriots steamed well, their mileage between repairs was not very high. These new types were reminiscent of London & North Western, rather than Midland, practice: two were 4–6–0s, a three-cylinder with 6 feet 9 inch driving wheels and a two-cylinder with 6 feet wheels; which were initially designated at Crewe as Claughton and Prince replacements, respectively. There was a 2–8–0 design to replace the successful LNWR G2 0–8–0s; and new versions of both types of passenger tank engines produced under the Fowler régime—the 2–6–4 and 2–6–2. Finally there was a 2–6–0 with 5 feet 6 inch wheels to meet the continued demand stimulated by the very successful Horwich engine. Actually this was the first of Stanier's engines. Although he had appreciated the high standard of Crewe boiler-making, he knew that the men had no experience of taper boilers; and the large taper boiler which he planned for his Pacific was better not undertaken without previous practical experience on a small boiler: hence the 2–6–0s. The very efficient boiler for which he was responsible was probably Stanier's greatest success. The detail design of the Stanier boilers was done by J. L. Francis, a draughtsman at Crewe who started his apprenticeship in the same month and year as Riddles, and to whom Stanier himself gives full credit.

Riddles, with his admiration for Great Western practice, welcomed this new range of engines, and his time with Stanier was more than happy. He found the new CME easy to talk to and only too willing to discuss, freely and frankly, all the problems with which they were faced. He would explain to Riddles anything he did not understand, without ever showing impatience at lack of knowledge, on the part of his subordinate; and on the other hand, if Riddles expressed views which were logical, Stanier would accept them. As Riddles says:

'He trusted everybody and his one fault, it is could be called a fault, was a lack of political acumen, and he could never imagine any intrigue against him. But we would talk of such matters and I think that I helped him to a certain extent. I suppose, having experienced first the Lancashire and Yorkshire taking over the London and North Western, and then the Midland taking over the lot, and the intrigue which resulted, I had developed a suspicious mind. I remember him returning from a meeting and saying, "They won't have it, Robert". The matter concerned was fundamental to his position, and I felt that if he gave way he would be surrendering a right inherent to the CME. I talked to the great man, explaining what I meant, whilst he listened staring down at his desk without saying anything. In due course we went home—I not knowing whether he agreed with me or not. In the morning he called me in and said, "It's all right, Robert, they've now agreed". This incident is worth mentioning as an indication of his great character. He never praised anybody for anything; good results he expected. On the other hand he could be cutting in his criticism. But he appreciated his staff, and as I got to know him better I realized that it was not what he said, but the tone of his voice which gave the clue to his feelings. I came to know him so well that I could tell from his face whether it was wise to say anything or nothing, and no man could have had a kinder or more understanding chief. Of course, as in the case of any person holding high position, there were those who did not entirely agree with his views, but he was regarded with appreciation and affection by all who came in contact with him, not only in Great Britain, but in India, America, and Canada. On one occasion in Canada he was addressing the Standards Committee and he told them that he had first heard of Standards when, as a young man, he received complaints from the Operations Department (Passengers) about the size of the hole in the lavatory seats. Stanier went off to the Joiners' Shop to investigate and was met by the foreman who said, "They are absolutely standard size, Sir," and, removing his bowler hat, he fitted it upside down into the hole!

'I became very close to the Stanier family and frequently visited Newburn, Rickmansworth (their home which was named after Churchward's house at Swindon) and they, too, were often at my home in Watford. In addition we met often on holidays in Scotland and Cornwall. Stanier was a great lover of Rudyard Kipling, and when he was not reading technical articles Rudyard Kipling came to his rescue. He was always reading and seldom, if ever, went out to such entertainments as the theatre or cinema. Indeed his "entertainments" were almost confined to meetings of the "Mechanicals", to which he was devoted, and he would delight in discussing technical problems at any time.

'In his latter days I visited him as much as I could, and invariably telephoned him when I went to London. I happened to telephone early on the morning he died (September 27, 1965), and his daughter told me that they had just found him. I took the first train and saw my old chief for the last time, lying peacefully at rest. I felt that it was a great privilege to be there at that time to do what I could to ease the burdens on his family.

'Some time later his daughter asked me if I would like the nameplate from the engine named after him. This was a treasure that I would indeed have loved to possess, but I thought that it should be offered to his son first. His son did in fact want it, but died himself before it could be sent to him. So now it is my proud possession, not only as a memorial to a great engineer, but as a constant reminder of a wonderful and great man.'

(This nameplate is on the wall of Riddles' workshop, opposite to that of *Edith Cavell.*)

This remarkable tribute by one great engineer to another is worth recording in full because it describes the character of both of them. And indeed the relationship between Sir William Stanier and Robert Riddles must be unique amongst locomotive engineers. They had the joint distinction of being the only persons to whom the Gold Medal of the Institution of Locomotive Engineers has ever been awarded 'For Outstanding Services in the Advancement of Locomotive Engineering'.

Sir William Stanier, on May 31, 1964, sent Riddles a copy of the biography of him written by Mr O. S. Nock.[1] It is endorsed to 'Robert Riddles, one of the principal members of the team that made the LMS story possible'; and the accompanying letter says that it was 'sent with my grateful thanks for our happy association'.

Stanier was an admirer of Churchward, both as an engineer and as a man. They were on very friendly terms and Stanier discussed with Churchward his designs for LMS engines. It is interesting to consider these three engineers. Churchward produced a fleet of locomotives for the Great Western which were a good twenty years ahead of those of any other British railway. But after Churchward retired no really new design appeared on the Great Western; all subsequent locomotives were developments of his own. The Castles were enlarged Stars and the Kings enlarged Castles: Halls were Saints with smaller wheels, and Granges the same engines again with wheels still smaller; Counties were Halls with big boilers; Manors were 4–6–0 versions of Churchward's 2–6–0s; Churchward's 2–8–0s hauled the heavy goods trains virtually unchanged from their introduction in 1903 until the end of steam; and the various classes of tank engines derived in

[1] Sir William Stanier—*An Engineering Biography*, by O. S. Nock.

the main from Churchward designs. The logical advance from Churchward's engines took place under Stanier on the LMS. His Pacifics were a proper step forward from *The Great Bear*, itself a development of the Stars, but which had come to a dead end after Churchward's departure; the Class 5 was a move forward from the Saint to an all-purpose two-cylinder 4–6–0 but, unlike the Hall, of a new and advanced design; the Jubilee could be considered as a three-cylinder descendant of the Star to provide a medium express passenger engine; the 2–8–0 was a modern version of the Churchward engine; and so on. For all these Stanier took Churchward's basic design of boiler and in due course improved on it by giving it a high degree of superheat. After Stanier retired, later engines on the LMS were developments of his own—and like the post-Churchward engines on the Great Western, they were not completely new designs (with the exception of Ivatt's six-coupled freight and tank engines). It was Riddles who produced really new designs for locomotives, building on Stanier's as Stanier had built on Churchward's. Riddles' Austerity engines were not, as some have claimed, cheap editions of Stanier's, but completely new engines derived from the Stanier legacy. The Austerity engines, again, formed the basis on which he built for British Railways. In the detailed design of these BR Standard engines, all the chief draughtsmen of the former major companies took a hand, but the Churchward/Stanier legacy was clear, and all had the Riddles development of the Churchward/Stanier boiler. All three engineers, indeed, stressed the importance of the boiler and paid particular attention to it. All three insisted on a minimum number of standard types with maximum route availability. All three refused to allow themselves to be immersed in detail; they would say exactly what they wanted and then let the draughtsmen get on with the detailed design. Riddles' particular contribution was perhaps his insistence on 'get-at-ability'—that is (having regard to different conditions in personnel, costs and fuel) engines with only two cylinders and everything on the outside, and uncovered for ease of maintenance and repair.

It is interesting to compare this Churchward–Stanier–Riddles development with the practice prevailing on other systems. The Great Western has already been mentioned. On the London and North Eastern, Gresley, great engineer though he was, embarked on a policy which was the very antithesis of the Churchward school. Though he was forced to follow Churchward's ideas to obtain the best results from his own locomotives, he never attempted any standardization. His engines were frequently 'tailor-made' to meet local conditions; and he designed a range of engine classes which were mostly fitted with three cylinders and a valve gear which was difficult to maintain. There was on the London & North Eastern Railway no general purpose mixed traffic engine, such as Stanier's Class 5, until Edward Thompson, who succeeded Gresley, produced his excellent B1 Class 4–6–0 with two cylinders, which was probably the most useful engine ever built for that line. Southern Railway locomotive policy was, of course, influenced by that company's rapid progress towards total electrification. But under his general direction, Maunsell had allowed Ashford and Eastleigh to go on building engines which were respectively South Eastern & Chatham and London & South Western in appearance and in many aspects of design; so that Eastleigh S15 Class 4–6–0s and Ashford N Class 2–6–0s appeared at approximately the same time to perform apparently identical duties. Bulleid stopped this, but he produced 0–6–0 freight engines (when other railways were building 2–6–0s) which were probably the ugliest locomotives ever to run in the British Isles, and Pacifics which were the most complex and difficult to maintain in proper order of any modern locomotives. Nevertheless, these same Pacifics illustrated the prime importance of the boiler; for their success in the haulage of fast and heavy trains was due solely, in Riddles' opinion, to the big boiler, which had such capacity that whatever happened to the chain drive the quantity of steam available overcame all troubles.

The new Stanier engines came out rapidly. The 2–6–0s led, of which 15 appeared in 1933 and the remaining 25 in 1934. The biggest delivery in 1934 was 82 of the three-cylinder 4–6–0s. In the same year there were built 20 of the two-cylinder mixed traffic 4–6–0s and 37 three-cylinder 2–6–4 tank engines for quick acceleration on the London, Tilbury & Southend line. The remaining Pacifics came in 1935, ten of The Princess Royal type and one which was turbine driven. Also in 1935 there were built no less than 205 two-cylinder Class 5 4–6–0 engines and the first 22 of the 2–8–0 heavy goods locomotives. There were also 8 2–6–4 tanks, but this time with two cylinders, and 74 of the smaller 2–6–2 tank engines. In addition, 48 more three-cylinder 4–6–0s were built in 1935, and the class was concluded in 1936 with a further 61. Other engines built in 1936 were 100 Class 5 4–6–0s, 42 2–8–0s, and 116 two-cylinder 2–6–4 tank locomotives. By 1936, then, Stanier had running 13 Pacifics, 191 three-cylinder 4–6–0s, 325 two-cylinder 4–6–0s, 54 2–8–0s, 37 three-cylinder 2–6–4 tanks, 124 two-cylinder tank engines, and 74 2–6–2 tanks. Over a period of four years, it was a massive effort. In the middle of all this building Riddles got another promotion on March 18, 1935, when he was made Principal Assistant to the CME.

The two-cylinder 4–6–0s gave excellent service from the start, but the three-cylinder 4–6–0s began their career with steaming trouble. They were, or should have been, the ideal engines for the Birmingham two-hour expresses. However, owing to shortage of steam there were a number of failures, and, without reference to the CME's department (Stanier was away) the Operating Department under D. C. Urie took them off the Birmingham expresses and transferred them to the Midland line and to duties which the Compounds, with their much lower tractive effort could manage easily. Riddles came back from leave as this transfer was taking place. His reaction was immediate: he gave instructions that jumper tops were to be removed at once and the diameter of the blast pipe orifice to be reduced from 5¼ inches to 4⅞ inches. For he had spotted that, far from the jumper tops being needed to reduce the blast, there was never enough of it: in fact, an arrangement that worked well with four cylinders on the Great Western was not suited to these three-cylinder engines of the LMS. The alterations were carried out on all engines within seven days. Riddles then gave orders that two Mechanical Inspectors attached to the London Office were, between them, to ride on all Jubilee class engines leaving St Pancras until further notice. The Inspectors were jubilant: the Midland drivers had never had such fine engines! When later the boilers were fitted with a higher degree of superheat the Jubilees became as efficient as any engines that Stanier designed.

The Class 5 Mixed Traffic 4–6–0s, or, as they were called 'Black Staniers' or 'Black Fives' (from their colour as compared with the red Jubilees), were developed from Stanier's 2–6–0s and were excellent engines from the start. But even they were not free from trouble. Whilst Stanier was in India in 1936–7, F. A. Lemon, Works Superintendent at Crewe, drew Riddles' attention to the boiler of one of the Class 5s. In order to save weight the firebox shell had been made of nickel steel plates with steel stays between the inner box and outer shell. A large number of these stays had fractured on both sides of the engine and the firebox was bulging both inside and out. Lemon said that this was the second engine of the class they had found like this. Riddles promptly gave instructions that boiler inspectors were to make a point of examining boilers in service at the first opportunity. Within 24 hours Lemon rang Riddles at Euston to say that his men had found seven more engines with this defect. Riddles immediately gave instructions that no more Class 5s were to go out of the sheds until they had been examined by boiler inspectors. He passed this information to the Motive Power Superintendent by telephone. (S. J. Symes, the Chief Stores Superintendent was actually acting CME in Stanier's absence, but he was sick.)

Riddles went home to a peaceful night's rest; but when he came back to duty the next morning he found that a monumental 'flap' had developed. Two Vice-Presidents were awaiting him at Euston, Ernest Lemon and Sir Harold Hartley. The latter had heard the news whilst at Oxford and had returned hurriedly to London. He was most disturbed at Riddles' action, as he believed that taking all these engines out of traffic would stop the line. Riddles, however, explained that if he had not stopped engines in this condition from being used and if in consequence there had been a fatal accident, he, as officiating CME, would have been criminally responsible. He could not therefore cancel his instructions.

Ultimately, investigation revealed that through a design error the stays concerned had been made with a centre portion slightly less in diameter than was desirable; when this was adjusted no further trouble occurred.

The first occasion on which I met Robert Riddles was early in 1937. I was then the Regular Army Adjutant of the London Corps Signals, a Territorial unit of Royal Signals. At that time we were seriously under strength and I conceived the idea of visiting various firms and organizations to try and make arrangements for attracting recruits. One of these was the London Midland & Scottish Railway. As with my other visits, I was kindly received, but without any helpful suggestions. (In fact these visits produced, as far as I know, no recruits, and we got them in an entirely different fashion: we started charging men £1 a head to enlist, which made it such a privilege to 'join that rather crack mob at Putney Bridge' that we were up to our war strength in six months and started accumulating a waiting list. With the funds thus accumulated we had tremendous parties for the NCOs, the men, their wives, and their girl friends.) However, I thought that the LMS might be able to supply a little publicity and I suggested that perhaps an engine might be named *Royal Signals*. This, somewhat to my surprise, was favourably received, and I was passed on to the people who dealt with these matters. There I was asked whether I would like a red engine or a black one. It seemed to me that a red one was more appropriate, in view of the traditional dress of the 'brutal and licentious', and I said so.

Matters were soon arranged. The LMS kindly provided the nameplates and the Royal Corps of Signals paid for the badges to be borne above them. The engine selected was Patriot class No. 5504 which was a rebuild or replacement of Claughton class 4-6-0 No. 1096 (built May 1920, rebuilt August 1932). The Colonel Commandant, Royal Signals, was to name the engine, assisted with a bottle of champagne provided by the LMS; the London Corps Signals were to furnish a Guard of Honour for the ceremony; and the LMS were to lay on a lavish lunch at the Euston Hotel, for which the menu cards were a joint production emblazoned with the Mercury badge of the Royal Corps of Signals.

The lunch, like all LMS special occasions, was indeed a lavish affair, rounded off with an excellent brandy and appropriate speeches. But I was getting worried about the Guard of Honour, and through the haze of cigar smoke and benevolence I made for the door. There I cannoned into an LMS man also leaving.

'Where are you off to?' he asked.

'To see if the Guard of Honour has arrived.'

'Damn the Guard of Honour. I want to see if the engine has arrived.'

It was my first encounter with Robin Riddles.

A short time afterwards we returned hospitality by inviting Stanier and Riddles to a guest night in the Mess; and Stanier presented us with a framed photograph of No. 5504 *Royal Signals*. (The engine has now alas been broken up, but she has bequeathed her name to a diesel locomotive working on the West Coast route.)

I was only fortunate enough to meet the late Sir William Stanier on these two occasions; but there was an indirect contact when I presented him through Riddles with a model of a 'Black Five' made in wood and cardboard. (A model which did not meet with my wife's whole-hearted approval, for I had purloined the roller out of the lavatory with which to fashion the boiler.)

On June 28, 1937, the telephone bell in my office rang. It was Riddles. 'We've got a new engine at Euston', he said. 'Would you like to come round and see it'. The story of that new engine belongs to the next chapter.

CHAPTER VII

From Euston to St Rollox

Riddles' move from Crewe to London was, he felt, rather similar to leaving school and going out into the world. Life in the Works had been very much of an enclosed existence, for the daily routine of a Works Manager was crowded with problems and activities, great and small, relating to the great acreage of shops and their hundred years of tradition. And those same shops were always there to be visited—either for specific purposes, or when the mood took one, or when there was nothing else demanding attention. In the shops there were a thousand things of interest and the men who were engaged in them to talk to. Crewe wrapped itself round its hierarchy as a regiment does its officers. London was quite different, and moving to the headquarters at Euston was, to pursue the military analogy, similar in its impact to that on an officer leaving his regiment for duties on the staff. The emphasis was on office work and paper and on contacts with other departments, rather than practical matters and the management of men.

Riddles now lunched daily with officers of his own level in other branches of the LMS. He had much to do with the financial side of the repair and construction of locomotives, and this brought him into close touch with the accountants and with the assistants to the Vice-President for Finance. He worked out with them a scheme to show the economies which could be effected by scrapping the older types of locomotives and replacing them with new ones; and the result of the acceptance of this scheme was that the Stanier 4–6–0 locomotives could be, and were, ordered in large quantities at a consequently low price.

On the financial side, too, Riddles became involved in a struggle with the Inland Revenue over a proposed revised system for taxing the railways. The Railway Companies maintained that their locomotives and rolling stock were always at from 90 per cent to

95 per cent of their capital value because of the methods adopted for repair. But at about this time an American journal, the *Railway Age*, published a statement that the American Interstate Commerce Commission had proved beyond all doubt that it was uneconomical to repair a locomotive that was over nineteen years old. As the railway case against the Inland Revenue was the subject of a court action it was important that the opposition did not have knowledge of this statement without there being evidence to refute it. Riddles, in his first year at Euston, was accordingly sent off to America to find out the evidence on which the ICC based their proof. He was accompanied by one of the assistants to the Financial Vice-President, T. Clifton, who, says Riddles, 'could make one believe anything by the time he had marshalled his figures'. The ICC were no match for the combined onslaught from Riddles and Clifton, and they were forced to agree that their proof rested on an insubstantial base. It related to an American practice of always sending a repaired boiler back to the engine from which it was removed, even if this entailed welding a new barrel on to an old firebox or vice versa—a most expensive way of doing things, and one which might keep an engine out of service for some weeks. The practice on the LMS was to treat the engine and boiler separately, and the locomotive building programme was based on an average of three new boilers for each locomotive during its useful life. No boiler was, in fact, regarded as belonging to an engine, and when during heavy repairs a boiler was removed, it was not necessarily returned to the same engine. The American 'proof', therefore, was based on the life of a boiler and not on that of an engine.

This was one of the many experiences that broadened Riddles' grasp of railway affairs; and the people he met who were engaged in other activities helped him to acquire that wider outlook, necessary to deal with matters for which a mind fashioned only by the necessarily parochial affairs of Crewe was ill-equipped. On many occasions, of which examples have been quoted in the last two chapters, he had to stand in for Stanier, with the consequent necessity of taking decisions or giving advice. One occasion, which had an amusing if for him rather embarrassing sequel, was the naming of the three-cylinder 4–6–0 engine *Silver Jubilee*. He had taken a great interest in the preparation of this engine, which was to be finished in black paint and chromium plate. He had found a firm which was prepared to do all, and in fact more than, the chromium plating for which he had asked. The engine, when she appeared at Euston for the naming ceremony by the Minister of Transport, was a lovely sight—dome, boiler fittings, hand rail, and lagging bands were a shining silver against the gleaming black paint. The day before the great occasion a message came from the Minister's office asking if someone could go and explain to him what he was to do. Both Stanier and the Superintendent of Motive Power being away, the task fell to Riddles. Sir Alan Mount the Chief Inspecting Officer, met him and took him in to see the Minister. The first thing that impressed Riddles was the amazing appearance of the room: the walls were sunshine yellow, the desk top and chairs were covered in blue morocco, and the telephone was blue to match. Having been waved into one of these impressive chairs, Riddles gave a brief explanation of the procedure. Acknowledging this with thanks, the Minister launched into railway spheres which were right outside Riddles' competence. 'Tell me', he said, 'how the railways are progressing.' It was a tall order, which swept magnificently right across the board. The Minister waited: Mount looked at Riddles; and Riddles sat for a moment in stunned silence, praying for guidance from Lord Stamp's guardian angel. He then burst into an impassioned exposition of the Railways' case. 'As you know, Sir, we are suffering severe competition from the roads: a competition which we think is unfairly weighted in their favour because, not being common carriers, the road haulage firms can pick and choose their loads and quote their own rates; whilst the railways, on the other hand, being common carriers, are bound to accept all traffic offered and to charge the standard rates'.

'I see,' said the Minister, 'I see'; and waited, obviously for further enlightenment. Riddles plunged on desperately with a tale of two ships which arrived at Hull, one laden with timber and the other with tomatoes, both of which cargoes were destined for the Birmingham area. The LMS were asked the charge for the tomatoes and quoted the standard rate, which was rejected. The rate for the timber, which was half that for the tomatoes, was accepted. But because the timber was in long pieces, empty wagons had to be marshalled between the loaded ones on account of the overhang. 'Now', said Riddles, in a flash of inspiration, 'if, Sir, we had been able to quote a reasonable price, the tomatoes could have been carried in those empty wagons at very little extra cost but at a good profit'. The Minister was impressed. 'Heavens', he said, 'I must look into this'. The deputation withdrew. Outside, Mount said in admiration, 'Riddles, you were splendid!' Triumphantly, Riddles marched off to tell F. A. Pope, the Commercial Manager how he had helped him. 'You did very well, Robert', said Pope kindly, 'but I think you should know that we never carry tomatoes in open wagons!' Feeling, and probably looking, like a tomato himself, Riddles returned to the more familiar world of the *Silver Jubilee*. It was some consolation that neither Mount nor the Minister had apparently thought that an open wagon was unsuitable for the conveyance of tomatoes!

The big new Pacific that Stanier had designed for the haulage of the fast express services between Euston and Glasgow was the logical development of the *Star-Great Bear-Princess Royal* series, and, like these illustrious predecessors, it was a four-cylinder engine. It differed mainly from the Princess class in having increased boiler capacity, bigger cylinders, larger coupled wheels, and two sets of Walschaerts valve gear instead of four. Furthermore, it was intended to be able to run at over 100 mph. The description of the new engine was released from the CME's office in May 1937. It said that the locomotive was one of a series of five, to be numbered 6220 to 6224, which were being built at Crewe Works. No. 6220 had just been completed and was named *Coronation* [1937 was the Coronation year of King George VI. In 1911, when King George V was crowned, the LNWR George the Fifth class 4–4–0 No. 5000 (the five thousandth locomotive to be built at Crewe) had been named *Coronation*], and the other engines were Nos. 6221 *Queen Elizabeth*, 6222 *Queen Mary*, 6223 *Princess Alice*, and 6224 *Princess Alexandria*. They were all to be streamlined in a form which had been designed by the Chief Draughtsman, Coleman, and finally approved after careful experiments with models in the LMS Research Department's wind-tunnel at Derby.

The decision to build these engines stemmed from the rivalry between the LMSR and the LNER, for the intense competition between the West and East Coast routes had survived the railway amalgamations of 1923. On the London & North Eastern Gresley's streamlined Pacifics had set up new records, including a maximum of 112½ mph with the *Silver Jubilee* express. Most locomotive engineers, certainly those of the LMS, heartily disliked this new practice of concealing the lines of a beautiful locomotive behind a streamlined casing, and Stanier loathed it. Nevertheless it did appear that for the sake of press publicity and public appeal it would be necessary to streamline the engines intended to haul the fastest services, if the LMS was to draw custom from the LNE, and the Directors accordingly so decided. Wind-tunnel tests had proved that streamlining had no worthwhile effect at speeds under 80 mph. No one bothered about side winds, though streamlining might even increase their pressure on the locomotive. In fact, it was only the publicity which could justify the £300 extra which was incurred in streamlining each locomotive. In addition, many parts of the engine which needed daily attention were covered up and this did not make streamlining popular in the running sheds.

The fixing of the streamlined casing presented quite a problem, as did also the access to the smokebox. There was a discussion on this latter difficulty between Stanier, Riddles, and Coleman. Coleman produced a scheme for the shape of the doors in the casing, but not a method of hinging them. Eventually, Riddles, using his building experience, suggested a solution and this was adopted. The streamlining fashion did not last long, and there was great joy when authority was given for it to be discontinued.

The larger coupled wheels of these engines were due to Riddles. He says: 'To my shame, I suggested to Stanier that the wheel diameter be increased to 6 feet 9 inches. My reasons were based on a remark by J. E. Anderson that beyond a given piston speed the locomotive lost considerably in efficiency, and, as presumably only light loads were to be hauled, longer legs would be able to run faster. This I suppose is true, but I had forgotten that the engine had to start from a stand; and could those big wheels slip!'

Riddles met me at Euston, when I arrived in response to his telephone call, and took me over the train and engine. The engine was painted 'Caledonian' blue with two broad silver stripes and, inside them, two narrow ones running from the front, horizontally, to the rear of the tender, and thence on along the sides of the blue carriages to the end of the train (Riddles, who had liked the livery of the Caledonian, suggested the blue). In front of the engine these stripes curved down to meet at a point. Riddles told me that the drivers, from the appearance of this front end, referred to the engine as the 'Butcher's Apron'! He also told me that on the following day engine and train were going on a test run to Crewe, but that he could not offer me a seat because every one had been allotted either to railway officials or the Press. As I was not expecting a seat, I was not disappointed, but I would have been had I known what was to be attempted. Riddles has recorded this epic journey as follows:

'On June 29, 1937, at 9.50 a.m. we set out from Euston with the new "Coronation Scot" train on its Press demonstration run. Again I was fortunate to be on the footplate, and with my diagrams laying down the postulated speeds, all was set to make an attempt on the world's maximum speed record at Whitmore, where, after a short rise, we entered on a falling gradient down to Crewe, 10½ miles away. We had decided not to pick up water from the troughs at Whitmore, and so avoid reducing speed. The exhaust was humming with a continuous roar like that of an aeroplane engine. The white mileposts flashed past and the speedometer needle shot up through the "90s" into the "100s" to 110–111–112–113–114 miles per hour; but beyond it—No! Basford Hall sidings 1½ miles away now; spectators from Crewe coming into view at the lineside, and the train still hurtling along at 114 mph. On went the brakes; off the regulator; but on we sailed with flames streaming from the tortured brake blocks. To my horror the signal was set for Platform No. 3 at Crewe, which has a reverse curve with a 20 mph speed restriction. We were doing 60 to 70 mph when we spotted the platform signal: down to 52 mph through the curve, the engine riding like the great lady she is: there wasn't a thing we could do about it but hold on and let her take it. And take it she did; with the crockery smashing in the dining car: past a sea of pallid faces on the platform; till we ground to a dead stand—safe and sound and still on the rails. We had set up a new world's speed record for the steam locomotive!'

As they entered that reverse curve, back in the train, F. A. Lemon, sitting opposite Stanier, said, 'We're for it now!', and put his feet up on the seat to steady himself. Some appalling misjudgment at Crewe had led to the train being switched to this difficult platform road, and it is probable that only the excellent de Glehn bogie (copied by Churchward from the French Atlantics and brought to the LMS by Stanier) had saved the train from disaster.

The LMS had now secured the speed record from the LNER, but, although the engine could probably have run a lot faster, there was no room to do it. Should the LNER, with a longer stretch of suitable track, regain the record, there was no possibility of a reply. And this is, in fact, what eventually happened. The return journey from Crewe to Euston was another distinguished effort. A speed of 100 mph was reached at one point and the 158 miles were run in 119 minutes—a shade under an average speed of 80 mph. Shortly after this the 'Coronation Scot' train went into regular service between London and Glasgow.

Riddles did not remain much longer as assistant to Stanier, after this memorable trip. Certain people in the LMS hierarchy were viewing his existing position with some anxiety in case it should develop into 'heir apparent' to the CME. He had now been Principal Assistant to the CME for four years and had frequently acted for him during his absences. But it had been clear to Riddles for some time that a brake was being applied to his upward progress. One indication of this had been the appointment of Symes to act as CME whilst Stanier was in India. Symes, one of the most popular officers of the LMS, did not take his appointment too seriously, and merely told Riddles to carry on and to let him know if there was any trouble.

The officially favoured successor to Stanier was C. E. Fairburn, who had been appointed Electrical Engineer of the LMSR in 1934. He had once caused some cynical amusement by remarking that in industry one spends 25 per cent of the time looking over the shoulder to see if anybody is after one's job, 50 per cent of the time in doing the job, and the remaining 25 per cent in looking round to see if there was any prospect of a better job! To ensure his succession in due course it was decided to make him Deputy CME, but this could not be done effectively without moving Riddles.

One evening, when he was about to go home Riddles was sent for by Sir Harold Hartley. Giving him a friendly greeting, Hartley said, 'We have decided to appoint Fairburn as Chief

Electrical Engineer and Deputy Chief Mechanical Engineer'. So what Riddles had feared had happened. He said, 'Yes, Sir Harold', and waited blankly. Hartley continued, 'We would like you to go to St Rollox in place of Ivatt and bring Ivatt to Euston as Locomotive Assistant.' Riddles expostulated, 'But Sir Harold, this is surely demotion for me.' Hartley tried to explain that it was nothing of the sort, and finally asked him to think it over and come back the next morning. Brooding miserably at home over this shattering blow, Riddles came to see that he had really no option but to accept, for he would not be allowed to retain his existing appointment, and if he refused Scotland there would be no future for him in the LMS; but at least he would try and make terms. Accordingly, when he re-visited Hartley the mext morning he said that if he was required to go he supposed that he would have to; but if it was logical to combine the duties of CME and CEE, it would be logical to make his appointment Mechanical and Electrical Engineer, Scotland. Hartley was apparently so relieved at his acceptance that he agreed immediately, and Riddles had at least, so he says, saved a bit of face. But in the bitterness of his disappointment he said, 'Sir Harold, in my experience there is a change of personnel in the railways every five years or so. I shall be back, but you perhaps will have gone'. He was immediately sorry that he made the remark, for Hartley got up from his chair and said, 'You may be right, Riddles, but good luck'. They shook hands, 'But', says Riddles, 'neither he nor I realized what a truly prophetic statement I had made, for eventually I was to have his job'.

There was an amusing sequel. The Chief Officer for Establishments had been told nothing about the scheme; and he was so angry that he arranged a rise in salary for Riddles, although he was already getting much more than Ivatt, and, in addition, he told Riddles that he could send in bills for carpets and curtains—a concession almost unheard of in railway circles.

Ivatt came to Euston to take Riddles' place, but the job was downgraded from 'Principal Assistant to the CME' to that of 'Principal Assistant to the CME (Locomotives)'. The way was now clear for Fairburn's appointment and he was appointed 'Deputy Chief Mechanical Engineer and Electrical Engineer'; a slight change, on Stanier's insistence, to the title proposed.

Above: LMS Class 5 4–6–0 No. 5258. *Below:* LMS streamlined Pacific breaking world speed record, June 1937. (Riddles can be seen on the footplate in the white coat)

By kind permission of British Railways

Above: L M S Pacific *Coronation* hauling the 'Coronation Scot'.

Below: Coronation being loaded on to the *Belpamela*, Southampton. (Note temporary track along the quay)

By kind permission of British Railways

Above: Press run of the 'Coronation Scot', March 18, 1939, and photographers taking pictures of it

Below: Display of locomotives at Washington Union Station. From *left* to *right*: LMS *Coronation*, B & O *Bullitt*, B & O diesel-electric, and Pennsylvania electric

By kind permission of British Railways

Above: 'Coronation Scot' and the BO diesel-hauled 'Capitol Limited' at Point of Rocks near the Potomac River

Below: 'Coronation Scot' on view at Dayton, Ohio

By kind permission of British Railways

Riddles left Euston and his many friends with great regret and went off to a job which, even though he felt that he was coming down in the railway world, was at least his own. He had dreams of a flat in Glasgow and a cottage by the sea. But the work soon gripped him and the vision of the seaside cottage (after initial enquiries had failed to discover any such cottage) soon faded. The Locomotive Works of the old Caledonian Railway no longer built engines, but were primarily responsible for repairing and maintaining those which were used by the LMS in Scotland. Urie and Ivatt had left a magnificent Works behind them and Riddles threw himself into the task of cutting down days under repair to the minimum. He started on the erecting shop, and in a few months half of it was being used for work other than locomotive repairs; and the time taken to repair a locomotive was brought down to six days, or forty-eight working hours. There were two roads for the two belts, and every day two locomotives went in for repair and two came out completed. This, known as the 'Six Day Plan', was unique and unequalled by any other repair shop in the United Kingdom. On the first day the engine was stripped and the various items carefully cleaned and examined. All parts which passed inspection were given a dab of green paint; if they were faulty they were marked with blue and sent for repair; and a red mark meant that they were only worth scrapping. The men got so enthusiastic about the new scheme that Riddles saw boiler-makers cutting smokeboxes off boilers, just received from traffic, whilst steam was still being blown down in the boiler. Engines came in for repair about every 60,000 miles, which was approximately every 2½ years. Boiler repairs were not so extensive in Scotland owing to the good soft water that was generally available.

Riddles was very impressed with the standard of foremen and men in the Works. They were all so keen that if he stopped and talked to them they would chat away without stopping the work they were engaged on. There were many interests too beside St Rollox: outdoor machinery at the ports, electric power and water at Gleneagles, and cranes at the Kyle of Lochalsh. Riddles began to enjoy himself. He had the old 'Caley' single, No. 123, repainted in the Caledonian Railway blue livery. But his time at St Rollox was destined to be short, and he was not to see the results of many things which he put in hand; for he had been selected to take the 'Coronation Scot' to America (which entailed many preparatory trips to England) and by the time he returned at the conclusion of that tour, the country was on the verge of war.

CHAPTER VIII

Tour in America

The American railroads had taken such a keen interest in the 'Coronation Scot' that they had pressed Lord Stamp to send a complete train to the United States to tour the Eastern part of the country and appear as an exhibit at the World's Fair in New York. Stamp agreed to this proposal and a train was selected which had just been built to the most modern and luxurious standards of the time, with a lounge car, a cocktail bar, telephone communication between each compartment and the kitchen car, and an extremely high standard of decoration and upholstery. The train consisted of eight coaches, of which the first six were three articulated pairs, each pair being mounted on three bogies. These were, in order, a corridor first brake, a corridor first, a corridor first lounge, a first diner, a kitchen car, and a third diner. This was the 'Coronation Scot' proper. The remaining two coaches were a sleeping car with six-wheel bogies and a club saloon mounted on four-wheel bogies. The train was completely air-conditioned, that is, for both cold and hot air. The general control thermostats were in the trunking through which the hot or cold air travelled, but in each coach there was a master thermostat that overruled these until the coach itself was at the required temperature. (In fact this air-conditioning system was to cause quite a lot of trouble. It may have been damaged in the sea journey, but in the United States the master controllers would not function, with the result that the temperature in the coaches rose to over 100 degrees Fahrenheit. It took Riddles a long time to find out what had happened, and in the end the master thermostats had to be cut out altogether.) The total tare weight of the train was 262 tons. The locomotive was numbered and named No. 6220 *Coronation*, but actually the name and number plates of the original 6220 had been changed with those of a newer streamlined Pacific, No. 6229 *Duchess of Hamilton*. The whole train, engine and carriages, was painted in the same style as the original 'Coronation Scot', but instead of blue with silver bands, the livery was Midland red with gold bands.

Riddles was detailed to travel to America in charge of the train, whilst Colonel K. R. N. Speir was to represent the LMS for publicity in the USA. Driver and fireman were F. C. Bishop and J. Carswell. Both had been presented with watches by King Boris of Bulgaria after that railway enthusiast monarch had been at the controls of the *Coronation*. The Crewe Works foreman, Master Mechanic F. W. Soden, had been selected to accompany the train with responsibility for maintenance. This new locomotive and the eight coaches were placed on view at Euston, and there was a lunch at the Euston Hotel at which Lord Stamp, as Chairman and President of the LMSR, formally bade farewell to the engine crew. Also present at the lunch were representatives of the men who had built the engine and carriages.

The only cargo vessels in the world which were suitable for carrying a complete train were the Norwegian 'Bel' ships, which had broader beams than ordinary freighters, clear holds in which railway tracks were permanently laid, and powerful derrick cranes. The 'Coronation Scot' was to be shipped at Southampton Docks in the *Belpamela*, registered at Oslo, diesel engined, and built by Armstrong's at Newcastle-on-Tyne. It was arranged that the locomotive and carriages should be loaded on board on or about January 20, 1939, and unloaded at Baltimore; whence they would be moved to the shops of the Baltimore and Ohio Railroad for assembly and preparation for the road.

The train was to visit thirty-eight American cities and towns and would cover 3,120 miles in the process. The tour was scheduled to start at Baltimore on March 21st and end at New York on April 14th. The train was then to be placed on show at the World's Fair which opened at New York on April 30th. The lengthy journey would entail running over the tracks of eight American railroads, and this was being co-ordinated by the Federal Interstate Commerce Commission.

Because most of the coaches were to travel as deck cargo, they were covered with a thick coating of wax to protect the red and gold paint from wind and salt sea spray. A special track was laid alongside the *Belpamela* and this was tested by a Southern Railway

Lord Nelson class 4-6-0. The 'Coronation Scot' engine and train were hauled 'dead' over the Southern Railway from Willesden to Southampton Docks on January 19th. The streamlined casing over the smokebox door, the coupling rods, and various other parts were removed from the locomotive before its journey for shipment and packed separately in crates.

Riddles, assisted by Soden, helped to supervise the loading and securing of the locomotives and carriages, which rested on their own wheels, though the carriage bogies were removed and loaded before the vehicles to which they belonged. The engine and tender and one coach were stored in the hold, having been lowered there by the *Belpamela's* own derrick crane of 150 tons capacity; the engine being secured on one side of the deck and the tender and coach on the other. The remaining seven coaches were disposed as deck cargo, securely lashed in position longitudinally. Some minor difficulties were encountered in loading, with the result that the ship sailed a few days late. At Southampton Docks a large white sheet inscribed with the legend 'Southampton Docks sends greetings to the USA by the "Coronation Scot"' was fastened to the side of one of the coaches.

The *Belpamela* sailed from the new Ocean Quay at Southampton on January 26th and should have reached Baltimore on February 14th; but she encountered such mountainous seas that she frequently had to reduce speed from 10 knots to 2. During three successive days she made only 200 nautical miles, and out of the twenty-five days that the passage eventually took, heavy seas and head winds were encountered on no less than twenty-one. The ship reached Locust Point, Baltimore, on February 20th—six days late.

Riddles, in the meantime, had crossed the Atlantic in the *Queen Mary*, whilst the train crew travelled in the *Aquitania*. All were at Baltimore to attend the unloading of the train. The unloading was carried out under particularly unpleasant weather conditions, with temperatures varying between 74 degrees Fahrenheit one day and 26 the next, and ice formed on everything. The coaches were lifted off their bogies and placed on B & O R R bogies on the quayside until their own were unloaded. The engine was brought up from the hold with British and American flags crossed on each side of the boiler. This crossing of the flags presented an unexpected difficulty. Riddles felt that as the engine was British, the British flag should have the place of honour; but the Americans insisted that their flag was always in the place of honour in their own country. This, to the onlooker, was on the left, but the heraldic niceties were unknown to the British observer, who was satisfied that his country's flag was on the right. It was February 24th before the entire train was assembled on B & O trucks at Locust Point and ready for movement. A Baltimore & Ohio engine then backed on and set off hauling the 'Coronation Scot' locomotive and coaches. At Bailey's Station, in south-west Baltimore, the train was run on to a 'Y' junction and reversed into the B & O Mount Clare Shops. Here the work of making the train ready was started. All the accessories which were removed from the engine before shipment, together with spare parts, were delivered to Mount Clare in a number of crates. An American pattern headlight had been built into the hood covering and the engine was also fitted with an American bell. During the unloading an American said to Riddles, 'It is strange that your locomotive fits our track.'

'Not, really,' replied Riddles. 'The first steam locomotive in America came from England and you had to make your tracks to suit it'.

As soon as the train was ready for the road, it was taken on an 'under cover' test run. Bishop, the driver, was feeling unwell at the time and the next day he was ill with pneumonia, probably contracted from the appalling weather. He went into hospital and was sick for most of the tour. In this emergency Riddles decided that he would take over the duties of fireman whilst Carswell became driver; though actually Riddles did most of the driving himself whilst Carswell did his proper job of fireman.

The first exhibition of the 'Coronation Scot' took place in the Mount Clare Shops on March 17th, when public officers and distinguished professional business men were given a preview of the train. A special trial run for the Press had been arranged for March 18th, and for this the day's work started at 6 a.m. and did not finish until 10.30 p.m. The first event was a group, arranged for the Press photographers, of the *Coronation* and some of the largest American express passenger locomotives, and staged in the yard adjacent to the B & O Camden Station at Baltimore. The 'Coronation Scot' then ran to Washington. The coal supplied for the locomotive was a nasty shock to Riddles. By British standards it was little more than slack; though it was adequate for the American locomotives which had fireboxes with mechanical stokers designed to burn it. The tender had to be refilled again at Washington, and Riddles reckoned that during the day they 'burned 11 or 12 tons of coal (or dirt)'.

The train was well photographed on the way to Washington. On arrival there it was backed into the Union Station, so that the *Coronation* stood beside and was dwarfed by the Baltimore & Ohio engine, *President Lincoln*. The driver (or 'engineer') of the latter leaned out of his cab and said, 'She's mighty pretty, but a little small, isn't she?'

The 'Coronation Scot' then started back in the direction of Baltimore, followed five minutes later by the blue, grey, and gold 'Capitol Limited' of the Baltimore & Ohio Railroad hauled by the *Bullitt* (as B & O men called the streamlined steam locomotive No. 5304). At Relay, Maryland, the 'Coronation Scot' was stopped on the eastbound track over the B & O's famous Thomas Viaduct over the Patusco River, which it spans in a graceful curve of eight arches. It was built as long ago as 1835 and is the oldest stone railway viaduct in the world. The 'Capitol Limited' drew up alongside on the westbound track, and these two trains filling up the curve of the old viaduct made an attractive spectacle for the Press photographers. Both trains were then photographed on the move from a flat car pulled by a 'less elegant engine' and crowded with camera men. The trains were then turned round and made a fast run back to the Washington Union Station. There the 'Coronation Scot' was inspected by the British Ambassador, Sir Ronald Lindsay; after which there was an official lunch in the station restaurant at which the LMS was host.

After lunch there was another spectacle for the photographers. An impressive array of modern express passenger locomotives had been drawn up at the far end of the station platforms. On the inside was the *Coronation*, with the *Bullitt* next to her, and then in order were a new streamlined diesel-electric engine, which regularly hauled the 'Capitol Limited' to Chicago, and a Pennsylvania Railroad 5,000 hp electric locomotive. These four engines moved slowly ahead in echelon.

In the afternoon the 'Coronation Scot' and the 'Capitol Limited', the latter hauled this time by a diesel locomotive, ran to Point of Rocks, where the Baltimore and Ohio line starts to run alongside the Potomac River, and made a number of stops for photographs. 'The Coronation Scot' was back in Washington about 4.30 p.m. and then returned to Baltimore. It had been a long day.

It was remarkable how much trouble the Baltimore & Ohio Railroad had taken to make the tour a success. In fact, it is probably fair to say that never in railway history has any train been the subject of so much publicity, so much hospitality, and so much courtesy. The Baltimore & Ohio Railroad has indeed a special claim to the affectionate attention of British railway men and enthusiasts.

The long and comprehensive itinerary which had been arranged for the 'Coronation Scot' is given below. The figures under 'Arrival' and 'Departure' relate firstly to the time by the 24-hour clock, secondly to the day of the month, and thirdly to the number of the month.

Coronation Scot Itinerary

Place	*Arrival*	*Departure*	*Railway*
Baltimore		2200/21/3	B & O
Washington, D.C.	2300/21/3		B & O
Washington, D.C.		2130/22/3	Pennsy
Wilmington, Del	2350/22/3	1145/23/3	Pennsy
Philadelphia, Pa	1220/23/3	2145/23/3	Pennsy
Lancaster, Pa	2310/23/3	1130/24/3	Pennsy
Harrisburg, Pa	1210/24/3	0030/25/3	Pennsy
Pittsburgh, Pa	0640/25/3		Pennsy
Pittsburgh, Pa		2130/25/3	B & O
Wheeling, W.Va	2350/25/3	1130/26/3	B & O
Columbus, Ohio	1530/26/3		B & O
Columbus, Ohio		1230/27/3	Big Four
Dayton, Ohio	1400/27/3	2200/27/3	Big Four
Cincinatti, Ohio	0010/28/3		Big Four
Cincinatti, Ohio		2100/28/3	Louisville & Nashville
Louisville, Ky	2355/28/3		Louisville & Nashville
Louisville, Ky		2030/29/3	Pennsy

Indianapolis, Ind	2330/29/3	1430/30/3	Pennsy
Terre Haute, Ind	1600/30/3	2130/30/3	Pennsy
St Louis, Mo	0100/31/3		Pennsy
St Louis, Mo		2100/31/3	Alton
Springfield, Ill	2335/31/3	1900/1/4	Alton
Chicago, Ill	1300/1/4		Alton
Chicago, Ill		2100/2/4	Michigan Central
Kalamazoo, Mich	0215/3/4	1330/3/4	Michigan Central
Battle Creek, Mich	1410/3/4	2100/3/4	Michigan Central
Detroit, Mich	0035/4/4		Michigan Central
Detroit, Mich		2100/4/4	NYC
Toledo, Ohio	2300/4/4	1230/5/4	NYC
Cleveland, Ohio	1515/5/4		NYC
Cleveland, Ohio		1230/6/4	B & O
Akron, Ohio	1400/6/4	2100/6/4	B & O
Kent, Ohio (one hour halt)			B & O
Youngstown, Ohio	2345/6/4		B & O
Youngstown, Ohio		1230/7/4	NYC
Erie, Pa	1500/7/4	2030/7/4	NYC
Buffalo, N.Y.	2230/7/4	2030/8/4	NYC
Rochester, N.Y.	2230/8/4	1330/9/4	NYC
Syracuse, N.Y.	1545/9/4	2200/9/4	NYC
Utica, N.Y.	2330/9/4	1320/10/4	NYC
Schenectady, N.Y.	1530/10/4	2100/10/4	NYC
Albany, N.Y.	2145/10/4		NYC
Albany, N.Y.		1200/11/4	Boston & Albany
Springfield, Mass	1500/11/4	2100/11/4	Boston & Albany
Worcester, Mass	2300/11/4	1230/12/4	Boston & Albany
Boston, Mass	1400/12/4		Boston & Albany
Boston, Mass		1230/13/4	N.Y., N.H., & Hartford
Providence, R.I.	1330/13/4	2100/13/4	N.Y., N.H., & Hartford
Hartford, Conn	0030/14/4	1330/14/4	N.Y., N.H., & Hartford
New Haven, Conn	1430/14/4	2100/14/4	N.Y., N.H., & Hartford
New York City	2300/14/4		

Riddles says that at every one of these towns and cities the Ford Motor Company generously put a car at his disposal, and, as soon as the train arrived, he would nip back from the engine to the sleeping car, slip off his overalls, and then call on the Mayor and invite him to open the exhibition.

The tour proper started on March 21st with the train being run on to a spur track on the west side of Baltimore's Camden Station produce terminal. At 10 p.m., on this first day of spring, an electric impulse was transmitted from the New York World's Fair, and this was the signal which started the 'Coronation Scot' on her epic journey.

Plenty of scope for trouble lay ahead, as Riddles well knew; for under these conditions even minor mechanical troubles could present major problems. The first of these came early with a broken spring bolt. This was made of manganese molybdenum, and nothing like it was available locally. Riddles, therefore, chose a valve spindle forging of similar tensile strength and had it turned down to make a bolt.

At Harrisburgh, before the first three days of the journey had been completed, the brick arch, which was of a new design, began to come adrift. As the Alleghany Mountains were ahead, Riddles had one of the two spare arches that they carried put in by the Pennsylvania Railroad boilermakers. But the work was so badly done that it was apparent they would have to put in the third arch. To Riddles it appeared that St Louis should be a big railway centre, and he wired there for help in the fitting.

Carswell had given the American Press his first reactions to United States railway conditions whilst they were at Philadelphia. He gave high praise to the American road bed; it was, he said, almost as good as the British. But he was scornful of the coal; the stuff they had been given at Baltimore was so dirty that they had had a hard job in cleaning the firebox. Between Baltimore and Wilmington a Pennsylvanian engine man had been in the cab to call the signals, but it had taken Carswell fifty miles to find out that the American signal for clear was white; with the polite implication that it had been hard to believe that such an archaic practice was exercised by a modern railway. From the unassailable pinnacle of a man who knew that his engine could run at well over 100 mph, he commented in courteous surprise that the

'Coronation Scot' had not been allowed to do over 85 mph in the United States.

Both the *Sun Telegraph* and the *Post Gazette* noted that when the 'Coronation Scot' left Pittsburgh 'the man at the throttle was R. A. Riddles'. At Louisville the *Courier Journal* remarked that the driver was R. A. Riddles, 'an executive and technical adviser of the London, Midland & Scottish Railroad'. The paper said that from 10 a.m. until dark thousands of people streamed into Tenth Street Station to see the train. It added that, 'standing a little to one side like the proud parent of a child prodigy, R. A. Riddles . . . said with modest untruthfulness that he simply couldn't understand at all why so many people came out to see a mere train'.

The Indianopolis *Star* reported that at times the crowd was so great that it packed every inch of the train shed and stretched into the main lobby of the station. It remarked that Riddles shovelled 10 tons of coal in the run from Baltimore to Washington and back and then went out the next day to play golf to get some exercise.

A Chicago *Tribune* reporter boarded the train at Indianapolis, to see how it compared with American streamlined trains, and travelled in it as far as St Louis. He thought it resembled the 'Broadway Limited', being the same shade of dark red with gold stripes running the length of the coaches at the level of the windows. He remarked that the train started so smoothly that the movement was hardly perceptible, and even the Pennsylvania man on board admitted to him that the drive was easy.

The *Greencastle Banner* of Indiana complained that the 'Coronation Scot' lacked the thrill in its movements and appearance that was anticipated. 'There was no noise nor bluster about it as it moved, such as is displayed by the common sort of trains with which Greencastle is familiar.'

The Terre Haute *Star* commented on Riddles taking over the job of fireman and said that 'This and the fact that the locomotive is constructed with such care that gaskets are unknown in the pipe fittings probably tells a better story of the British than all the excellent fittings and arrangements for comfort on the train'.

Near Terre Haute, a few miles east of Brazil, the train passed through the farm of Bruce McCormick. The Terre Haute *Tribune* said that he and his brother stood to attention beneath a huge British flag flying from a 30-ft. stripped tree. As it passed them, the 'Coronation Scot' slowed down and the driver sounded the whistle in salute.

The help available to instal the new arch at St Louis was disappointing. A boilermaker and his coloured mate presented themselves as the only staff available. Three of the back rows of bricks had fallen from the arch into the firebox, forming a fused mass. It was then 1 a.m. and departure was scheduled for 9 p.m. that day. Nevertheless the arch had to be changed; but it was no easy task to remove the old one and get it out through the drop-gate, when the bricks were not only white hot but had to be broken up individually before they would pass through the small opening.

By 4.30 a.m. the faulty arch had been removed, and Riddles went off to the hotel, where only the magic name 'Coronation Scot' saved him from being turned away at the door. There he had some sleep before rising again at 8 a.m. for breakfast. Then he went off to call on the Mayor and get him to open the exhibition.

To allow the engine to cool down, they waited till 2 p.m. before starting to fit the new arch, but even then there was still a pressure of some 50 lbs. of steam in the boiler. Under such arduous conditions Riddles, Soden and the boilermaker (the coloured mate refused) went into the firebox. Riddles says:

'Three hours of heaving lumps of firebrick, some weighing 25 lbs. and others up to 80 lbs., inside a firebox with 50 lbs. of steam pressure all round is an experience not to be forgotten!'. However, the job was finished by 5 p.m., and an hour or so later the fire was in again and going well. He then went off for a hot bath, followed by a rump steak washed down with a bottle of champagne. Little aware of difficulties on the engine, 20,000 people, according to the St Louis *Daily Globe Democrat*, had been passing through the train in the Union Station. At 9 p.m. they steamed out of St Louis and Riddles was driving the train to Springfield, some 120 miles away. Near a place called Plainview they were running at from 70 to 75 mph when up went a red flare, which was an American method of indicating an emergency stop. On went the brake, the regulator was shut, and the train came to a stop some 200 to 300 yards from a motor car that had missed its way and straddled the track. Riddles drew the train up to the obstruction and got down out of the cab to meet a very white-faced individual who said that he could not move the car. The train crew got him back into his seat gave the car a hefty shove to help the engine, and, with a smell of burning rubber as the skidding wheels scraped over the rails, a very scared but relieved citizen of the United States vanished into the darkness.

At 1.35 p.m. the 'Coronation Scot' arrived at Springfield, Illinois, where Riddles went to bed after what he says, 'might fairly be described as a busy day'. At Chicago, on April 2nd, Riddles received an American locomotive whistle which was presented by the Model Railroad Builders of America. The presentation took place in front of the 'Coronation Scot' with a Baltimore & Ohio diesel locomotive on the adjoining track. Riddles was now continually encountering the first manifestations of that diesel revolution that in such a few years was to sweep steam locomotives away from all of America's track. As yet it was only a trickle; the first modern-type main line diesel locomotive in the world had been sold by General Motor's Electro-Motive Company to the Baltimore & Ohio Railroad in 1935, and in 1939 this company still had a monopoly in supplying the as yet very limited demand. Riddles was not very impressed. It seemed to him that many miles of running would be needed before savings from the increased thermal efficiency made up for the vastly increased cost in capital and maintenance as compared with a steam locomotive.

A special stop, intended to be of one hours duration, was made at the town of Kent in Ohio, because it was the home town of a colourful figure, Charles C. Green who was Director of Promotion in the World's Fair organization and who was travelling in the 'Coronation Scot'. For his use the First Class dining car had been transferred into a World's Fair exhibition coach with miniature displays provided by various American companies. According to the Kent *Courier Tribune*, between 2,500 and 3,000 people were waiting to board the train and it said that the 'Roosevelt High School Band and the Portage County Recreation and Sons of the Legion bugle and drum corps participated in the parade through downtown Kent to the depot where the Scot lay at anchor'. Green was given an official reception and there was a dinner arranged in his honour at which Riddles, in the first speech of the evening, said that the LMS had sent its crack streamlined train to 'bring Charley Green home'.

Bishop had rejoined the train at Akron, but the bands and maroons which greeted the train at Kent upset him and he was sent on that night to Buffalo for further rest and treatment. He finally joined to take up his driving duties at Syracuse on April 9th.

The *Courier* of Buffalo said that the train had been travelling at moderate speeds due to lack of American braking power, but had been let out on a few occasions, due, it was said, to 'Mr Riddles, the executive turned fireman who is reported to be a "speed demon" '. The Rochester *Democrat and Chronicle* quoted Riddles as saying, apropos of his temporary job, 'Somebody had to shovel. A bloody dirty job, I'll say, but we managed.' On April 10th, approaching Schenectady, the 'Coronation Scot' ran under a bridge over which, at the same time, was passing the Twentieth Century Limited' on its way from New York to Chicago. According to the Boston *Herald*, a crowd estimated at 18,000 jammed the concourse at South Station, standing patiently in line for hours to see the 'Coronation Scot'. Up to the time the train arrived at New York some 425,000 visitors had passed through the train and about another 100,000 had been turned away. In Cincinatti alone 27,000 people had visited the train.

At one stage of the tour complaints were made about a mysterious banging in the sleeping car whilst it was running. A preliminary examination failed to disclose anything wrong. It was only when the Federal Inspector, who was riding on the train, said that the car would have to come out, that it was discovered that the body had settled down too far on the springs as a result of the buffeting by rough weather during the Atlantic crossing. This was put right in less than 15 minutes by adjusting the springs—to the amazement of the American fitters, for under their vehicles there were only solid spring links which could not be adjusted.

On the arrival at New York Riddles says, 'I must admit that I was thankful to see the World's Fair ground and relieved that we had got to it all in one piece. I had lost seven pounds in weight—but we were there!' By the time the Fair was over more than 2,000,000 people had inspected the train.

Because of the great success of the train the Fair authorities and the American Railroads asked if it could remain on exhibition in 1940, provided that they undertook to pay all expenses for reconditioning. The LMS agreed only because the War had started.

Riddles returned to the United Kingdom early in May 1939. It had been intended that he should go back to America later in the year to bring the 'Coronation Scot' back to England, and that he should do this at the end of a months holiday in America and Canada which the grateful LMS authorities had granted him. All arrangements had been made for a trip through the Rockies to Vancouver and his passage had been booked in a suitable ship; but owing to the outbreak of war the promised holiday never took place.

After the end of the Exhibition the engine was stored in the shops of the Baltimire & Ohio Railroad until a suitable opportunity should arise for its return to England. When he subsequently visited the United States in 1940 on ministerial business, Riddles was able to arrange for its return to help meet the shortage of locomotives in the United Kingdom. The carriages, however, were used as a club for Army officers and did not come back to England until after the end of the War.

Just after the test run at the start of the tour, Riddles received a letter from the President of the Baltimore & Ohio Railroad, in which he said, 'I have no doubt that we could place you as a driver on one of our important trains if you should ever decide to leave your country and take up active railroad duties in ours'. Coming from one of the most respected Railroad Presidents and one who had been very helpful to them, it was a compliment that Riddles greatly appreciated.

CHAPTER IX

Ministry of Supply

Riddles found St Rollox a little tame after the excitements of his tour in the United States. Nevertheless, it was with hopes of returning there before long that he got down to his job again. At that time he was living in a flat in Glasgow; the city seemed oppressive and he had a longing to get out into the country. He was delighted to find a new block of flats being built in the lovely countryside which comes so close to Glasgow. He chose one of the flats and moved in. With a golf links close by, life, for a few days looked good. But it was not for long: on the afternoon of Saturday September 2, he was sitting in his new flat when the telephone rang. It was Sir Harold Hartley. 'Riddles', he said, 'would you come up to London to-night. I have made an appointment for you with Sir Harold Brown at the Ministry of Supply for 10.30 to-morrow morning. Come and see me at Euston afterwards.' He rang off.

One of the steps taken, as Great Britain moved reluctantly towards war, was the establishment of a Ministry of Supply. It had been intended that this Ministry should be responsible for the provision of all equipment for the three Services, but the Admiralty and the Air Ministry had protested that only they were capable of dealing with naval and aircraft construction respectively. Thus, when the new Ministry came into being in August 1939, it was responsible only for equipment for the Army and for the procurement of raw materials.

When, before the War, the re-armament programmes were taking shape, Engineer Vice-Admiral Sir Harold Brown had been appointed Director-General of Munitions Production at the War Office. When the Ministry of Supply was set up he was transferred to it as Controller-General of Munitions Production. It was then decided that the purchase of transportation stores for the War Office should be added to the responsibilities of Sir Harold Brown's department, and that a Directorate of Transportation Materials should be formed with a railwayman as its Director. Sir Harold Brown wrote to Sir Harold Hartley and asked him for a nomination. Hartley recommended Riddles.

At the interview, which took place on the day war broke out, Riddles was asked by Sir Harold Brown if he would take charge of and form the new Directorate (the title of which was changed on September 27 to Directorate of Transportation Equipment). He agreed, and went back to report, but feeling a little deflated that the LMS should have apparently been so ready to dispense with his services. He travelled back to Glasgow that night, cleared up his desk, shut up his flat, and travelled back to London again the following night. At Euston he met at breakfast R. C. Bond, who was to take over from him in Scotland. He then went to the Ministry of Supply and was ushered into the new office which was awaiting him as Director. Everything was completely new—desk, bookcase, arm chair, and even inkstand, pens and pencils. But the desk was bare of any papers, and Riddles sat down at it feeling somewhat lost and wondering what to do next. After a time the door opened and someone came in and put a file down in front of him, saying, 'You might like to read this.' He had started!

The responsibilities of the new Directorate were wide, for they included, all types of equipment, not only for railways, but for docks and harbours, inland water transport, and the War Department fleet. The day after Riddles' arrival, there was a knock on the door and in walked Colonel (later Brigadier) A. S. Redmond. Riddles says, 'He had come as my Deputy, and I can still see his look of surprise when he saw his comparatively young chief. What a joy he was and what a lot I owed to him. He knew the Whitehall "establishment", its methods and its channels, and would side-step its objections by means unknown to me. With his help we began to build'.

Demands soon came in and there was no more idleness for Riddles. Locomotives were wanted, not only for the British Expeditionary Force, but for Africa and Ceylon, and India wanted wagons of all types. In July 1939 the Ministry of Transport (the Ministry of Supply not having yet been formed) had announced that the War Office would need locomotives for use overseas. As an instalment to meet this requirement it was agreed that the

Great Western Railway should supply 100 0–6–0 freight locomotives. The engines selected were the remarkable little 2301 class of goods engines designed by William Dean in 1883, which had already given outstanding service in the First World War. Their popularity was due to their simplicity, comparative power, and a light axle load which permitted their use on the flimsiest of track. In replacement of them the LMSR and LNER had agreed to lend the GWR 40 0–6–0s each, whilst the SR had undertaken to help by preparing some of the engines for service on the Continent. (All the locomotives which were sent to France in 1939–40 were lost during the subsequent operations.) But although perhaps adequate for the immediate needs on the Lines of Communication of the small British Expeditionary Force, they were much too small for the haulage of the heavy ammunition and supply trains which would ultimately be required. The idea of a standard type of locomotive for military purposes occurred first in the war of 1914–18, when the excellent 2–8–0 heavy goods engines designed by J. G. Robinson were selected for service overseas. They were probably his best engines, despite the more glamorous appeal of his Atlantics and Directors, and their only rivals were G. J. Churchward's 2–8–0s for the Great Western. However, a great disadvantage (which would also have applied to the Great Western engines) was that when, after the end of the war in 1918, large numbers were available to run on the railways of the United Kingdom, the width over the cylinders prohibited their use over a very large proportion of British lines, particularly those which became the LMSR. The GWR, with its large construction gauge, could take them, and the LNER could make use of them over a great many of their routes.

The demand facing Riddles for locomotives was urgent, and he had to make up his mind as to how he was to get the quickest possible delivery. He realized that owing to the urgency he would have to select an existing type. He was tempted by the Robinson type on account of the large numbers already available in the country; but he rejected the idea, because over the years they had been modified to suit the particular railways on which they were working and they could no longer be considered as constituting one standard class. There would therefore have to be new building based on an existing class of heavy freight engines. There was no question in Riddles' mind as to which was the most suitable. Stanier's 2–8–0s were well tried and had given excellent service on the LMS. Riddles accordingly went off to see Stanier and asked if he would help with drawings, patterns, press blocks, etc. and if he would agree to T. F. Coleman, his Chief Draughtsman, discussing the problems with the North British Locomotive Company. Stanier agreed readily.

As a result, a total of 240 Stanier 2–8–0 locomotives were ordered for the War Department, though only 208 were actually built—158 by the North British Locomotive Company and 50 by Beyer-Peacock. In addition to these, however, 51 engines which had been built for the LMS were transferred to the War Department, making a total of 259.

The orders were placed in December 1939 and the North British Locomotive Company delivered the first engine in May 1940. From then on deliveries averaged two to two and a half a week. But by the time that the first engine was ready the Allied front had been broken and the British Expeditionary Force was fighting a desperate rearguard action in its withdrawal to the coast. The circumstances of the time may have been responsible for the inaccuracies contained in an announcement by the Ministry of Supply's Press Office on May 21, 1940. It said that Mr R. A. Riddles, Director of Transportation Equipment Ministry of Supply, was to take delivery at the North British Locomotive Company's Works at 10.30 a.m. on Friday May 24th of the first of several hundred locomotives ordered by the Ministry of Supply for use with the BEF in France. The locomotives ordered, it said, were of the standard LMSR and GWR 2–8–0 type, modified to suit conditions for operating in France. At that particular moment the BEF (this author amongst them) were all too rapidly bequeathing their Continental railway lines to the Germans, and in a day or two were to be more concerned with destroying the equipment they were being forced to leave behind than with receiving more from the United Kingdom! However, the notice was happier in its concluding statement that, 'The engine was chosen because of its simplicity of design, its known behaviour in service, its freedom from troubles in running, and its flexibility in that its gauge dimensions are such that it can run anywhere in this country or abroad'. One detects the hand of Riddles in this sentence. The requirement for simplicity in design would have ruled out Gresley's three-cylinder LNER 2–8–0 and gauge dimensions in the United Kingdom militated against the selection of the GWR 2–8–0.

The collapse on the Continent caused the automatic cancellation of an order to meet a request by the French for 10,000 covered wagons of continental design. Riddles, having arranged the sale of the wagons without approval by the appropriate authority, was a bit scared when it came to signing a contract with a French financial attaché for some £7,000,000. However, before the order was anything like finished the deterioration in the military situation prevented any further shipments.

With the stoppage of work on the wagons and the easing of the demand for locomotives, Riddles began to get restive. He thought he should go back to the railways and said so. The response was to give him lots more work and responsibility. He became Deputy Director-General Royal Engineer Equipment and head of a greatly enlarged Directorate dealing with all engineer stores and material. There were now ten branches of which only one dealt with railway locomotives and rolling stock.

The cancellation of part of the order for Stanier 2–8–0s was due to the Allied defeat on the Continent. Engines being built or completed were directed to the Middle East, where more locomotive power was badly needed. 228 were despatched, of which twenty-three were lost at sea by enemy action. The remainder were used in Persia, Palestine, Egypt, and the Western Desert. In addition to the Stanier engines, Riddles did acquire in 1941 ninety-one of the Robinson 2–8–0s and these were also sent to the Middle East; none ever came back to England. Both classes did excellent service and the Robinson 2–8–0s could be seen running on the same duties as the Stanier engines and sometimes partnering them on heavy double-headed goods trains.

For his greatly enlarged Directorate Riddles, naturally, drew largely on the railways, taking people he knew. As Secretary he chose an old LNWR man, C. Dennett, who had been with him in his days at the Crewe Progress Office. Dennett, a great organizer who was dedicated to his work and was absolutely loyal to Riddles, soon picked up Civil Service rules and procedures and never put a foot wrong. For the purchasing side Riddles asked for, and got, some very good men from the Stores Department of the LMS, one of whom, C. F. Havord, he had had as an excellent secretary of a Policy Committee. At the head of his Transportation branch was a Swindon-trained man, A. F. Walters, who had such charm of manner that he could extract help or knowledge from anybody. Riddles only had to ask him to do something and it was as good as done. On one occasion Walters telephoned Sir James Milne, General Manager of the Great Western and a Member of the wartime Railway Executive Committee, for help of some sort. Milne agreed, and in expressing his gratitude, Walters said, 'You know, Sir James, Mr Riddles is very pleased with what you are doing'. 'Indeed!' said Sir James. Receiving this news of his patronizing appreciation of one of the most formidable figures of the railway world, Riddles says that he felt a little faint, but adds that Walters could get away with anything.

Gradually Riddles acquired a first class team and the Directorate acquired an enviable reputation of being able to provide anything. Riddles would not tolerate an 'It's not my job' attitude. His instructions to all members of his staff were that if they were asked a question, whether it was their job or not, they must provide the answer or else tell the questioner where and how to proceed.

Redmond left the Directorate after two years and was relieved by another sterling character, K. C. Stacy Hatfield. Riddles had been very careful to select for his staff only men who had a detailed knowledge of the jobs which they were to undertake. But the first rate technician is not necessarily the best person to send to a high level meeting. Hatfield, with his charm of manner and polite firmness, was ideal. At one such meeting an exasperated General said, 'Mr Chairman, I do not know what is in the mind of the Ministry of Supply'.

'What do you say to that, Hatfield?' asked the Chairman.

'I think, Mr Chairman,' replied Hatfield, 'that it is a good job he doesn't'.

As the Directorate expanded, so it began to deal with needs other than those of the Army. It provided all Services, for instance, with cranes, industrial internal combustion engines, and bridging. As regards the last, the Christchurch Experimental Station was under the direct control of the Directorate. Riddles had difficulty in getting a suitable bridge. The Inglis bridge of the First World War could only carry light loads. To increase its capacity, Inglis specified a tougher steel junction box; but it proved impossible to cast this to the narrow limits necessary. Mr Bailey, who was then chief designer at Christchurch, made a sketch for a suggested bridge on the back of a foolscap envelope which was shown to Riddles. He liked the idea and approved the construction of a trial bridge in mild steel. The trial was successful, and the bridge was demonstrated to the War Office. They saw its possibilities immediately, and plans were put in hand for a number to be made of an alloy steel, to obtain strength with lightness. Riddles was asked what the bridge should be called. 'Well,' he said, 'we already have the Hamilton and the Inglis; I think we should call this the Bailey', and so it became. Demand was so great that production was eventually astronomical. Colonel P. K. Benner, in charge of bridging, was found one morning by the cleaners asleep over his papers. But this dedication to the job was general throughout the Directorate.

The Bailey Bridge was found capable of providing all sorts of combinations to meet the needs of different loads and situations. Trials of these combinations were not always, however, immediately successful. At Christchurch the first Bailey suspension bridge was erected, an imposing structure some 400 feet long, which Riddles was invited to open formally. He did so by cutting a ceremonial tape and driving over it in a 'Jeep'. Memory of the event was somewhat marred by the appearance in his office the following morning of a pale-faced Brigadier who said, 'I am sorry to report, Sir, that the bridge you opened yesterday has fallen down'. However, it transpired that there had been no failure attributable to the bridge. A junior officer had been instructed to replace the temporary tower supports with those intended for the permanent structure. He promptly removed the temporary supports first—and the bridge collapsed!

Choosing the right man was always a problem. When Riddles took over the production of industrial internal combustion engines, the obvious approach would have been to ask one of the firms for help. But the best man from the point of view of a firm would not necessarily be best suited for a job in the Ministry. Seeking an answer to the problem, he was introduced to a consultant, W. A. Tookey, from whom he asked advice. Tookey came back in a few days and said that the only man he could think of was himself. Riddles asked him how old he was, and on Tookey replying that he was just seventy, he said that he could not ask for a man of that age to be taken on. Tookey was indignant. 'I'm fit enough,' he said. Tookey got the job and did it magnificently. He got on well with both the manufacturers and the 'customers' and, by intensive standardization, increased enormously the output of internal combustion engines. Thus there were a number of different standard types, and in each of these types there were standard variations according to their usage. One type, for instance, had seven different crankshafts to suit seven different purposes. Crankshafts, indeed, became such a specialized problem that a separate branch dealt with them.

Cranes required an entirely different treatment. The crane section dealt with every type of crane for a variety of users—the three Services, railways, ports, and firms engaged on Government business. The Directorate had a Crane Allocation Committee at which users and manufacturers met each month to decide priorities and the possibilities of meeting them. It was soon apparent that the normal existing types of crane would not meet the demand. Riddles felt that the urgent requirement for mobile cranes could only be realized if a large quantity of specified types and sizes were ordered, giving any one firm only a particular size or capacity so that they could mass produce. He believed that a first order of 1,000 mobile cranes would be necessary. But going home he remembered with some alarm that on the LMS there had been only about a dozen mobile cranes for the whole system. Worried, he went over his figures, but they still came out at 1,000; and as the war went on and the demand for mobile cranes grew, his forecast proved right.

Wharf or dockside cranes were another potential demand, for, as the tide of battle swept forward it was clear that cranes would be needed in large numbers for the rapid rehabilitation of damaged ports. Production capacity was limited and standardization was necessary if there were not to be a number of different types each of small numbers. To solve the problem Riddles held a meeting with the manufacturers and said that he must have a standard dockside crane. This should be diesel-electric with electric motors which could use the ship's power supply if necessary. Messrs Stothert & Pitt undertook the design and Riddles made them the parent company. Eventually they, with the help of all the other manufacturers, were turning out six-ton cranes at the rate of one a day and did, in fact, complete 365 in one year. (This was Riddles' first encounter with Stothert & Pitt. After he retired from railway service he was to become the firm's Chairman.)

The jerrican provided the Directorate with one of its more interesting jobs. The German petrol containers captured by the British Army in the Western Desert were so good and so superior to their own cans that they asked if they could be supplied with a similar pattern. A blue-print of what came to be known as the jerrican (after the British soldier's name of Jerry for his German opponent) was sent to Riddles together with a requisition for two plants to manufacture them in Egypt. Riddles asked for six cans as samples and an order for one million cans so that a suitable layout could be developed. He then called the manufacturers together and told them that it was to be a cooperative job. A lot of problems had to be solved, for 'Coming as it did', says Mr M. M. Postan (*History of the Second World War—British War Production*), 'at the height of industrial mobilization, it raised considerable difficulties.' But the cans were duly produced, a layout was arranged for continuous manufacture, and the plants were sent to Egypt for manufacture there. When half the order was finished Riddles handed over the business to the Directorate whose responsibilities included containers. By the end of the War some 50 million cans had been produced at, says Mr Postan,[1] a maximum rate of half a million cans a week.

Another unusual task was the production of the Mulberry harbour piers and pontoons, of which the first prototypes had been ordered from the Ministry of Supply in September 1942.[1] The first trial took place in the Solway Firth of this ingenious idea which was to play such a large part in the invasion of France—an idea which was very dear to Churchill, for in May 1942 he had stressed to the Chief of Combined Operations the need for piers specially designed for beaches.[1] During the trial a storm blew up which made actual passage on the pier impossible, but the artificial harbour behaved extremely well. Fortunately an Army cinema

[1] History of the Second World War—British War Production.

'bove: The 'Coronation Scot' at Chicago

3elow: Riddles receiving an American locomotive whistle from the Model Railroad Builders ·f America

3y kind permission of British Railways

Above: The 'Coronation Scot' at speed near Kalamazoo, Michigan, April 1939
By Kind permission of British Railways

Below: Riddles in the cab of the *Coronation*
By kind permission of The Times-Union Democrat & Chronicle

unit which was present was able to take very good pictures. Riddles was present when the film was shown to Churchill, and the latter was so impressed that before he left he ordered another four miles to be made.

These were some of the tasks that were undertaken by the very versatile Directorate of Royal Engineer Equipment. The demands on it were tremendous; all of them were technical and for many of them the Directorate was responsible for design. They had to use whatever sources of supply they could get, against the competition from armaments, aircraft, naval vessels, etc. Locomotives were in competition with tanks. Lord Beaverbrook, who became Minister of Supply in June 1941 and to whom, Mr Postan says, tanks were now 'the thing', once sent for Riddles and accused him of ordering locomotives after he had written to the firm concerned telling that they would get no more orders for locomotives. Riddles said, 'You did not send me a copy of your letter, Sir.'

'Well', he replied, 'they will not get the order for locomotives.' Riddles comments, 'But in fact they did, and we got the locomotives.'

Riddles says that the Beaver, as he was always known, was adept in giving a job to a person other than that to whose department it belonged. This usually enraged the latter so much that he either worked harder or gave up. He sent for Riddles one day and told him that he wanted him to take charge of supplies to Russia through Persia, and to fit up a room with detailed maps of Persia on the walls and all the available books on the country where he could come and talk to him. 'But', says Riddles, 'he never came'. However, having got the room ready, he started on this new task, which really belonged to another Directorate. 'Nobody', he says, 'argued with the Beaver, but you had to stand up to him.'

A large number of the Stanier 2–8–0s had been fitted to burn oil fuel before being sent to Persia. They were very successful in the cooler months of the year but they encountered an unexpected 'snag' in the abnormally high temperatures of the South Persian plain. This area is one of the hottest in the world, and Andimeshk, the main British military centre at the time, is reputed to be the world's second hottest town (I must plead ignorance as to the identity of the hottest!). Whether Andimeshk's reputation is deserved or not, the Royal Air Force recorded an official shade temperature on one day of 135 degrees Fahrenheit. This sort of temperature was too much for the LMS cold water injectors and they refused to work. Davis & Metcalfe hot water injectors had to be sent out immediately. In a cold water injector the steam supply is admitted to a nozzle, the diameter of which is gradually reduced so that it attains a high velocity, shooting into a water space which surrounds the nozzle. The cold water immediately condenses the steam, but in doing so the steam gives the water sufficient impetus to carry it into the boiler against the latter's pressure. If the water is hot the condensation is a slower process and a more complex method has to be used for transferring the velocity of the steam to the water.

LMS type 2–8–0s were not only built for the War Department. Riddles' choice of them led to their being adopted in December 1941 as the standard heavy freight engine which was to be built to satisfy the Railway Companies' immediate needs, so that there would be a reserve to draw on for further commitments overseas. On completion of existing orders for their own types, therefore, the principal railway works began building these LMS engines. Of works other than LMS, Doncaster built 50, Darlington 53, Swindon 80, Eastleigh 23, Ashford 14, and Brighton 93.

Any account of Riddles' non-military activities at the Ministry of Supply must mention the Army 'fleet'—an assortment of target towing launches, tugs, and other small vessels, used solely for army purposes. Serving under him for the supply of this miscellaneous flotilla was a retired Vice-Admiral. On one occasion Riddles was taken down to the depot at Greenwich from Westminster Pier in a towing launch fitted with two 500-hp Maybach engines and having a speed of 40 knots. To his huge delight Riddles was piped aboard this vessel, causing no little excitement amongst the crowd overlooking Westminster Pier.

CHAPTER X

Austerity Locomotives

As the war developed and plans for the invasion of France began to mature, it became apparent that a very large number of locomotives would be required; for the Germans would evacuate or destroy as many as they could and Allied bombing would eliminate much of the rest. It was clear to Riddles that the Stanier 2–8–0s could not be built in sufficient quantities, firstly because of the number of man-hours required for each, and secondly because of a serious shortage of much of the material used in them, particularly steel casting and forgings, twenty-two tons of the former alone being incorporated in each engine. The Robinson 2–8–0s again entered his mind, and he wondered whether their use in bulk would after all be practicable. But again the lack of standardization amongst these engines appeared to present an insuperable objection, even if he could have got them all away from the Railway Companies. The Chief Mechanical Engineers of the railways were aware of his difficulties, and one day Sir Nigel Gresley called on him with the offer to transfer to him almost immediately all the Robinson 2–8–0s in LNER possession, if Riddles would undertake to replace them as early as possible with new engines of Gresley's three-cylinder O2 class 2–8–0 design. Riddles says, 'I was profuse in the thanks with which I refused the offer, but I felt that I could build two, or two and a half, of the type I had in mind for every one of the O2 class, apart from the difficulty of finding the materials'.

Riddles now began planning an entirely new engine, which should have the minimum of attachments, be easy to prepare for running, have maximum accessibility, and be simple to maintain. The Railway Companies were rather concerned at this change in policy, and so was the Ministry of Transport because they had visualized the LMS 2–8–0 being built in large numbers and bought at bargain prices after the War. Sir Alan Mount, the Chief

Inspecting Officer of Railways, telephoned Riddles and told him that no CME of a British railway would ever allow the engines he was proposing to build to be used in the United Kingdom. Riddles retorted, 'I don't mind if you push them into the sea after we have won the war'. (In fact, hundreds of these engines were used in Great Britain and overseas, and they were amongst the last steam locomotives on British Railways to be scrapped. They were liked by both operating departments and works for their ease of running and maintenance.) Riddles went ahead with his plans for the new engine. Mainly to silence early criticism, he gave it the name of Austerity (already associated with wartime economy standards) and published the reasons which lay behind economies in the design.

The firm which was to cooperate with Riddles in the design and development of the Austerity engines was the North British Locomotive Company. It has now, alas, ceased to exist, but in the days of steam it had strong claims to be regarded as the greatest of all British firms building locomotives. It was founded in 1903 by the amalgamation of three Glasgow locomotive manufacturers: Neilson, Reid & Co. (Hydepark Works), Dübs & Co. (Glasgow Locomotive Works), and Sharp, Stewart, & Co. (Atlas Works). The oldest of these was Sharp, Stewart, and the largest Neilson, Reid.

The firm of Sharp, Roberts, & Co., as it then was, built its first railway locomotive in 1833 at the Atlas Works in Manchester. It soon established a name for itself in the railway world. The 2–2–2 Sharp Singles, built between 1837 and 1857, eventually numbered about 600. For reliability and appearance they had few rivals, and they acquired a considerable reputation on the Continent—so much so that they were copied by André Koeklin for the Alsace Railway and by Stehelin & Huber for the Orléans Railway. The firm's title changed to Sharp Brothers in 1843, and to Sharp, Stewart in 1852. From the 1840s till 1854 Sharp's Chief Draughtsman was a German, Charles Frederick Beyer who, says Mr George Dow in his book *Great Central*, enjoyed the enviable reputation of never having designed an ugly engine. He left Sharp's to found, with Richard Peacock (who had been Locomotive Superintendent of the Manchester, Sheffield & Lincolnshire Railway) the famous locomotive firm of Beyer, Peacock.

In 1888 Sharp, Stewart, & Co. moved to Glasgow, where they

took over the principal interest in the Clyde Locomotive Works from W. M. Neilson, and renamed them the Atlas Works, after their Manchester establishment.

The Hydepark Works were founded by W. M. Neilson, and seem to have been operating by 1837. At first the firm was known as Mitchell & Neilson, but it became Kerr, Mitchell & Neilson in 1840, Neilson & Mitchell in 1845, and Neilson & Co. in 1855. In 1858 Henry Dübs was appointed Manager of the Hydepark Works and soon after they were moved from Hydepark Street to Springburn. In 1863 Dübs left the firm to set up his own locomotive works and was replaced by James Reid as managing partner. In 1876 there was a disagreement between Neilson and Reid, resulting in the former leaving the firm. In 1884 Neilson established the Clyde Locomotive Works which were taken over by Sharp's. In 1898 the title of the original Neilson's was changed to Neilson, Reid & Co.

Dübs & Co. opened the Glasgow Locomotive Works in 1903, moving there from the original establishment in Polmadie. In 1864 William Lorimer had entered the service of Dübs & Co., and in 1867 he became principal assistant to Henry Dübs and was made a partner in 1875. After the death of Henry Dübs he became managing partner.

In 1903, at the suggestion of Hugh (later Sir Hugh) Reid, senior partner of Neilson, Reid & Co., the three companies amalgamated as the North British Locomotive Company. William (who became Sir William in 1920) Lorimer was the first Chairman with Hugh Reid as Deputy Chairman and Chief Managing Director. William Lorimer's eldest son, also William, became the third Chairman, and his son, W. D. Lorimer, was later joint Managing Director. It was the North British Locomotive Company, which as stated in Chapter IV, built the first fifty Royal Scots so rapidly for the LMS. These engines came straight off the drawing board, with no time for trials. But either due to the rush or to the incorporation of certain Midland features, or both, there had been troubles. Water circulation in the boiler was bad, and bogies, wheel centres and springing gave trouble. (It was, in fact, only after Stanier rebuilt them with modified cylinders, altered valve gear, improved boiler, and de Glehn bogie, that they became the best 4–6–0 express passenger engines in the British Isles.)

Now Riddles was to attempt another rush job in conjunction with the North British Locomotive Company and again to assay a locomotive straight off the drawing board. But there could be no repetition of the Royal Scot deficiencies and this would entail his close personal supervision at every step. The Chairman of the North British Locomotive Company, with whom Riddles was to deal so much, was W. Lorimer, the son of Sir William. Each week for many weeks on end Riddles travelled to Glasgow on the Friday night. There he spent Saturday in the North British Locomotive Company Drawing Office and Sunday with James Black the Technical Director. He says that he drew the Drawing Office staff and the Works together in a manner never experienced, even in the North British Locomotive Company. If a component was designed which was difficult to manufacture the design was altered.

The Austerity engine had some relation to the LMS 2–8–0 because the outline scheme had been got out by F. G. Carrier, a draughtsman who was section leader in the development and design branch of the Derby drawing office. (Carrier was, indeed, largely responsible for what Stanier's and Riddles' engines looked like.)

For ease of manufacture Riddles had chosen a parallel boiler with a round top firebox, rather than the intricate and expensive Churchward pattern of taper boiler with Belpaire firebox. He almost eliminated steel castings, cutting down the 22 tons needed for the LMS 2–8–0 to only 2½. Cast iron replaced steel castings for all except the driving wheel centres. The leading truck wheels were rolled in one piece, and the tender wheels were chilled cast iron. But here Riddles slipped up. He had seen heavy freight wagons in the USA with these sort of wheels and observed how badly they behaved when over-braked. He had arranged for the percentage of brake leverage to be lowered on the tender to avoid this, but he had not allowed for the prevalent practice of drivers, when descending a bank with loose-coupled stock, to apply the steam brake fully, screw down the tender hand brake, and then release the steam brake. This had most unfortunate results, for the tender wheels were badly damaged. Fortunately this happened in the early days and there was time to substitute rolled forged wheels. (He heard afterwards that the Chairman of one of the Railway Companies had said that the leading truck wheels were cast iron!) Another trouble was that a slight 'fore-and-aft' movement caused the built-up draw bar buffer between engine and tender to collapse, but stronger control springs remedied this. It was apparent that hostile and critical eyes were watching his engine, but he did not bother too much because he was sure that he was on the right lines.

With vivid memories of the trouble he had experienced with crossheads on the LMS Pacifics, Riddles chose the Laird pattern with twin bars above the piston rod (which were also much cheaper to manufacture). As stated earlier, he dispensed with boiler lagging and used air insulation only between the boiler and steel clothing sheets. There were two outside cylinders, 19 inches by 28 inches, driving the third pair of coupled wheels, which were 4 feet 8½ inches. (It is of some historical interest that the diameter of the coupled wheels was the same as that of the driving wheels of Stephenson's *Rocket* and also of the railway gauge.) The valve gear was Walschaerts and, of course, outside. The boiler pressure was 225 lbs. per square inch, the grate area was 28·6 square feet, and the weight of the engine in working order was 72 tons, of which 62 tons were available for adhesion. Cab and footplate arrangements were simplified as far as possible.

Riddles never approved of undue emphasis on thermal efficiency. The basis of his engines was a boiler which would meet all the demands made of it. He says, 'Whether or not they would burn a pound or two more a mile than a more sophisticated engine, I regarded as the unrealistic preoccupation of the theorist, because in practice a good driver and fireman could save pounds if given a free-steaming engine.'

Riddles anticipated a great deal of criticism of the Austerities and he remembered that his old friend Charles S. Lake, Editor of *The Railway Engineer*, had once said to him that the first thing that anybody noticed about an engine was the chimney. If, therefore, one wished to deflect criticism, the best way to do it was to design a ridiculous chimney. The critics would then concentrate on that and forget about the rest of the engine. So Riddles put an absurdly small dumpy chimney on his engine which was three inches lower than the rest of the boiler mountings. In diverting criticism from the more controversial points of the design, the results were highly gratifying. Nevertheless, he was too much of an artist for the chimney to be really ugly, and the Austerity, unlike Bulleid's dreadful looking 0–6–0 for the Southern Railway, was a handsome engine. (This chimney had an unexpected bonus because when Riddles designed the later and larger 2–10–0s for the War Department it was just right for the most exacting restrictions of the British loading gauge.)

Riddles awaited the appearance of the Austerity locomotive with a certain natural anxiety. On November 23, 1942 he wrote to W. Lorimer, Chairman of the North British Locomotive Company, asking him to do all in his power to get the first engine out by the end of the year at the latest and if possible before Christmas. He added:

'I think you are aware of the antagonism of the Chief Mechanical Engineers to this engine, and our one hope of getting it running on the British Railways is to produce it at a time when they are desperately in need of power and will be forced to take it in hand. When this has been done, I am quite sure that the locomotive itself will prove so effective in service that all their criticisms will be overriden and it should be accepted with joy by the operators'. He went on to say that the first American locomotive was arriving in a few days and there was a big 'poohbah' to greet it, in which he was joining, mainly as a return for the welcome given to the 'Coronation Scot'. But he did not want the shade of its arrival to last too long and obscure the impact of the home-made Austerity.

Lorimer replied on November 25th, saying that since he had received Riddles' letter he had been in discussion with those of his staff concerned in the matter; but he did not think there was any possibility of steaming the first Austerity engine that year. He said that there had been difficulties over supplies, material, labour, and existing contracts.

But it was not long after the end of the year, because the first of the Austerity 2–8–0 locomotives was handed over at the North British Locomotive Company's Works on Saturday January 16, 1943. It was inspected by Sir Andrew Duncan, Minister of Supply, and among those present were Sir William Douglas, Permanent Secretary Ministry of Supply, Sir Geoffrey Burton, Director General of Mechanical Equipment, Riddles, W. Lorimer, and J. Black. The engine had been built in five months from the date of placing the order, and after all the parts had been delivered it had been assembled in ten days. The speed with which it was built was, in fact, a record for the North British Locomotive Company. The previous record had been five months from the time the designs had been received. According to the *Glasgow Herald*, William M'Pherson, the driver, said, 'This is the first time I have had a cushioned seat for my work, and altogether I have never handled a better engine'.

Production of the Austerities was rapid, because, owing to the simplicity of the design and the use of more readily available materials, thousands of man-hours were saved and time lost waiting for parts was drastically cut. Whereas the LMS 2–8–0s were being built at the rate of two to two and a half a week, the Austerities were turned out more than twice as fast, for from five to six were produced each week, and with the help of other manufacturers this rate eventually rose to seven. And, as a result of Riddles' visits, week-end after week-end, to Glasgow, and although the engines were produced straight off the drawing board, there were no teething troubles, apart from the quickly remedied errors over the tender wheels and draw bar buffer. It is only necessary to remember the Royal Scots to appreciate what a triumph of design this was. But it was an anxious time, for the engines to be built without prototypes or trial were eventually to number, not 70 like the Royal Scots, but no less than 935—second only to Ramsbottom's DX goods as the largest class of British locomotives ever built. 'The decision to do this', Riddles says, 'required courage, because there were so many critics of my policy who were only awaiting a chance to "pounce".' (Of the 935, 545 were built by the North British Locomotive Company and 390 by the Vulcan Foundry.) Since these engines were turned out in advance of military needs, no less than 450 were lent to the Railway Companies, and did excellent service before they were withdrawn for shipment from October 1944 onwards. Of these 350 ran on the LNER, 50 on the LMSR, and 50 on the SR. The LNER got their first engine in February 1943, and it made its first run from a Glasgow goods yard on a freight train on the West Highland line. The engines were an immediate success. In his book *Steam Locomotives* Mr O. S. Nock quotes a very senior railway officer at York who loved North Eastern engines but told him that the 'WDs' were by far the best they had ever had.

The War Office were extremely pleased with the new engine, so much so that they asked Riddles to produce a locomotive which should have the same tractive effort as the Austerity but with only 13½-ton axle load instead of 15½. This was a problem. Riddles first thought of a 2–8–2, but he felt that he would lose adhesion and decided that a 2–10–0 was the right answer, and that it should have a bigger boiler with a wide firebox. To enable it to run through a 4½ chain curve, he decided that the centre coupled wheels should be flangeless and those on each side have flanges of reduced thickness. This caused some trepidation at the North British Locomotive Company, but Riddles insisted. He had curves laid out and calculated that with a wider wheel tread all would be well. The first of the engines to be turned out was taken to St Rollux shed, and was just about to go through a sharp curve when a ganger, who happened to be there, ran up waving his arms and protesting that the engine could not go through as the curve was much too sharp. But it went through all right without even the usual 'grind' of a 2–8–0. Riddles says that they had got, in effect, the equivalent of an articulated engine, because, with the slight flexing of the frames, the 2–10–0 was very easy on curves.

After the War, when the LMS was asked to take over some of these 2–10–0s, the Civil Engineers objected to using them until they could test the 'throw-over' on a 1 in 8 curve at a station platform. The argument about this went on for some time, and Riddles believes that there was difficulty in finding such a condition. He got tired of waiting and telephoned General McMullen and asked him if he would make a test at Longmoor, where he knew there was a 1 in 8 crossing in the station. This was a Saturday morning, and by the Monday he had received a highly satisfactory chart of the complete test. He presented this to the Chief Engineer, who then agreed to the engines being used.

The demand for the 2–10–0 arose because the 2–8–0 was not considered suitable for the haulage of very long and heavy trains over light, improvised, or imperfect track. As compared with the 2–8–0, the 2–10–0 had a considerably longer boiler and with the wide firebox the grate area was increased to 40 square feet. A rocking grate was provided. Riddles decided on a more orthodox lagging of the boiler because of the extremes of temperature to which it might be subjected. Underneath the steel clothing plates were asbestos mattresses, laid against the boiler barrel and firebox.

Riddles' 2–10–0 class, the first of which was completed by the North British Locomotive Company in June 1944, was undoubtedly one of the masterpieces of British locomotive engineering. Major-General D. J. McMullen, Director of Transportation, wrote to Riddles on February 15, 1945 saying that he had just come back from a visit to the British Liberation Army and had to let him know how excellently the Austerities and 2–10–0s were doing. 'Everyone', he wrote, 'loves the 2–10–0. It is quite the best freight engine ever turned out in Great Britain and does well on even Belgian "duff", which is more like porridge than coal. The 2–8–0s have trouble for steaming on this muck alone, but if they can get 25 per cent of Dutch lump coal mixed with it they do all right'. He added that it was amazing to trundle along on a 2–8–0 Austerity only three miles from the German front line. In Nijmegen station the shell bursts in the battle area could be seen from the footplate, 'So your products are well up into the fighting area, often ahead of the medium artillery positions'. On January 4, 1946 McMullen wrote again to Riddles saying, 'I have yet to see in Europe anything to touch your 2–10–0, weight for weight'. A total of 150 of these engines were built, all by the North British Locomotive Company.

Riddles had returned to the LMS by the time the first of the 2–10–0s began to appear. Stanier was still CME (though he retired early in 1944), and one Saturday he walked into Riddles' office. 'Bad luck, Robert,' he said. Riddles was at that moment being told by Walters, from the Ministry, that seven or eight of the 2–10–0s had been stopped at Peterborough with broken stays in the firebox. He asked Stanier how he knew as he had only just got the information himself. Stanier replied that it had been given out over the 'tin can'. This was the name given to the daily telephone conference, held under the authority of the then Railway Executive, between operating officers of all railways and at which were reported and discussed arrangements for traffic control, untoward incidences, etc. Riddles says:

'Stanier was not malicious—in fact I do not think he could be—but I knew that many others did not like my having produced new designs. I replied lightheartedly (without, of course, intending it unkindly), "It reminds me of the crisis with the Class Fives and their broken stays". We said no more, but, in spite of my assumed lightheartedness, I was very worried. It was a Saturday, so I was back early at my home in Watford and immediately got out my car and drove off to Peterborough. Just as I arrived at Peterborough station, to enquire the whereabouts of the running shed, I saw coming round the corner Tom Lawson, the North British Works Superintendent. He had a broad grin on his face when he saw me. "What is it Tom?" I asked. "The bloody fools have been tapping the flexible stays!" he replied. I breathed a sigh of relief, and how we both enjoyed it! But no correction was announced over the "tin can"!'

(Normally, when stays are tapped with a hammer they give a ring if they are sound and a dull thud if they are not. But flexible stays, being linked together, also respond to a tap with a dull thud.)

The Directorate of Royal Engineer Equipment controlled all locomotive manufacture, and this included Beyer Garratt locomotives for Commonwealth countries, Colonial territories, and the lines of communication of the forces operating in Assam and Burma. Many other requirements were met by using or adapting existing types of, for instance, both steam and diesel shunters. In response to a War Office request for steam shunting locomotives of the same capacity as the LMS Class 3 Freight 0–6–0 shunting tank engine, Riddles chose the Hunslet standard shunter, a very fine little 0–6–0 saddle tank and much better than the LMS engine cited. But, as in the manufacture of the Austerities, the materials available and the nature of its employment would necessitate extensive modification before it would be suitable for mass war construction. Steel castings and forgings, for instance, would have to be replaced by fabricated parts, the wheels would have to be of cast iron and increased in size, coal and water capacity would have to be increased, brass tubes would have to be replaced by steel, etc. Riddles asked Mr Edgar Alcock, Chairman of the Hunslet Engine Company, to come and see him. This meeting was followed by discussions between the Directorate and Hunslet and Riddles went himself to Leeds to visit the firm. Delivery of the modified locomotives which resulted began at about the same time as the first of the Austerity 2–8–0s made their appearance. Eventually 377 of these shunting engines were built by six different firms.

The high regard which the North British Locomotive Company had for Riddles was marked by the firm's presentation to him of a golden key to their Hydepark Works.

CHAPTER XI

Return to the LMS

In the New Year Honours List of 1943 Riddles had been awarded the CBE for his distinguished services in the Ministry of Supply. His time there had greatly broadened his outlook, for, as recorded in the previous chapter, he had had to deal with all types of what the Army regarded as engineer equipment, most of which was required in a hurry and the production of almost all of which was hampered by shortages of material and labour. In the course of his work he had to deal with many people—soldiers, civil servants, industrialists, and others—who were complete strangers to the railway world, and whose methods of working and outlook on life were entirely different. He had had great authority over a wide range of manufacture and, far from being a mere departmental head, he had been personally concerned in technical detailed planning. At times he had felt the difficulties and frustrations so overwhelming that he had applied to see the Second Secretary concerned, with a view to returning to the railway.

The Second Secretary, whom the author is privileged to number amongst his friends, was later, as Sir George Turner, to be Permanent Under Secretary of State for the War Office. Sir George is a very remarkable man and a keen student of human nature. Behind his desk at the Ministry of Supply there hung a picture frame into which it was his practice to insert a picture calculated to influence a visitor in the way he desired. When Riddles visited him the frame held a very large photograph of an Austerity engine. When this caught Riddles' eye, says Sir George, there came into his face the sort of fatuous expression with which a very young man regards the female object of his affection. The purpose of the visit would be forgotten and Riddles would be diverted into discussing the features and performances of his engine.

However, the time came when Riddles found that all design

work had been completed and prototypes tested and approved. There remained only production, (though admittedly this was no small problem) and he had a feeling that the war must come to an end before long. When, therefore, Sir William Wood, President of the LMS, came to see him and suggested that he should return to the Railway, he fell for the idea with some feeling of relief. Creative work in the Ministry of Supply seemed to be at an end, and the LMS was, after all, his career.

Lord Royden, Chairman of the LMS, now spoke to the Minister about Riddles' future, with the result that the Minister sent for Riddles and asked him what he would like to do, adding that Lord Royden had told him that it was in his interest that he should rejoin the LMS. Riddles agreed, though now with a great deal of reluctance. In fact, it was a decision which he still regrets and wishes he had stayed until the job was finished.

Riddles' departure from the Ministry of Supply was regretted by many people. Sir George Turner says that if they gave him a job to do they never needed to worry, for he would not only do it but do it extremely well. His complaints about his difficulties, Sir George regarded in an entirely different category to those of certain other persons with whom he came into contact, and which he likened to a dog which a traveller across the United States encountered in Texas. The train drew up at a station in a flat plain almost devoid of any vegetation and nearby was a dog, with its head raised to the sky, howling piteously (the 'piteously', emphasizes Sir George, is important). The traveller asked why the dog was howling piteously, and was told that it was because he was sitting on a piece of cactus. The traveller looked at the large areas of ground devoid of cactus and asked why the dog had to sit on a piece. 'Because', said his informant, 'he likes to howl piteously'.

Riddles returned to the LMS on August 1, 1943 in the very important position of Chief Stores Superintendent, taking over from S. J. Symes. On his departure from the Ministry, Admiral Sir Harold Brown wrote to Sir Harold Hartley saying that he had no doubt received the thanks and appreciation of the Ministry through the appropriate channels for the outstanding services that had been rendered by Riddles, but he felt impelled to write a personal note to Hartley to convey his gratitude for having suggested his name in the first instance. He continued, 'He has done a magnificent job and a very big one, which has continually grown until it is one of the biggest jobs in the Ministry. He has not only carried out any work entrusted to him with the utmost efficiency, but has earned the respect and affection of all who have worked for him'. It was a great tribute from a very great man.

There had been changes in the LMS since Riddles left. Lord Stamp, who had combined the duties of both Chairman and President, had been killed in an air raid, and the two offices, as indicated above, had been split. From the start of hostilities all the railway companies had been placed under the then wartime Railway Executive, which consisted of the General Managers, or equivalent, of the four big companies and London Transport. There was, in addition, a Mechanical and Electrical Engineers Committee, under the chairmanship of Sir Nigel Gresley, consisting of the four Chief Mechanical Engineers and the Chief Electrical Engineers of those companies which had them. This committee dealt with all matters concerning locomotives, rolling stock, and workshops.

Most of the management staff of the LMS had been moved from Euston to a large house called The Grove about two miles north of Watford. The greater part of the CME's staff moved to Derby under Stanier's Deputy, Fairburn, and Stanier himself set up an office with a small staff at The Grove. In April 1941 Gresley died and Stanier succeeded him as Chairman of the Mechanical and Electrical Engineers' Committee.

At the end of 1942 Stanier, whilst still retaining the Chairmanship of the above Committee, was seconded to the Ministry of Production as one of a team of three scientific advisers. He continued officially as CME but, owing to the limited time he would have to devote to railway affairs, Fairburn was appointed Acting CME. At the end of 1944 Stanier resigned from the LMS and early in the following year Fairburn was appointed in his place. Ivatt remained with him as Principal Assistant.

Towards the end of Stanier's time as CME, the most noteworthy locomotive event was the rebuilding of the Royal Scots. One of the Jubilee class 4–6–0s had been rebuilt with a much larger taper boiler with 250 lbs. pressure and a double blast pipe and chimney. A second engine was rebuilt in the same way, and these two were

Above: The 'Coronation Scot' at the New York World's Fair, 1939
By kind permission of British Railways

Below: LMS Type Stanier 2–8–0 built to Riddles' requirements for the War Department
By courtesy of Bryan H. Jackson

Above: Group in front of an Austerity 2–8–0 locomotive at NBLC Works (Riddles is fourth from the right)

Below: Riddles and Black with Austerity Class 2–10–0 *North British*
By courtesy of Bryan H. Jackson

more competent locomotives than the Royal Scots. At this time the boilers of the Royal Scots were getting old and their Midland-type built-up smokeboxes were continually leaking air and ruining the draft. It was accordingly decided to rebuild all of them with these new boilers. Since Stanier had effectively left and Fairburn was not a steam locomotive engineer, Ivatt became responsible for supervising the rebuilding of these engines in 1943.

Riddles was particularly fitted for the job to which he was now going. Firstly, and most important, he was extremely interested in it; secondly, he had an intimate appreciation, from his own past experience, that the supply of material at the right time and place was of paramount importance. The proper organization of such supply had played an essential part in his reorganization of Crewe and St Rollox Works and in the work he had been called upon to undertake at the Ministry of Supply. Hours, days, and even weeks, could be wasted in waiting for materials; and it was not only time that was wasted for time is expensive, and costs could soar.

His deputy in the stores department was A. W. Norman, who, he says, was a genius at the job and should rightly have had the appointment. However, when Riddles left, he was able to secure Norman's promotion to succeed him. Norman, he says, knew better than any Engineer the nature and use of the enormous variety of materials used by the railway. To Riddles he was one of the most loyal of friends that he had ever had and he never showed any resentment at a new chief being brought in over his head.

In running the stores department, Riddles left Norman to arrange the purchasing contracts and all the details connected with them. His own contribution, true to character, consisted initially in getting out of the office to see what was happening. He found the conditions of storage dreadful and promptly gathered all the storekeepers together to institute action. He reorganized the bin storage system and the stores themselves and introduced proper methods of stock-keeping. He then increased considerably the usable stock, but disposed of unwanted and obsolete articles; thereby avoiding any increase in the total value of the stock. All this was done fairly rapidly, for he was helped enormously by the tremendous enthusiasm of the storekeepers. A great deal of this was due to Riddles' personal impact: never before had a Stores

Superintendent been amongst them so much, and Riddles' own enthusiasm was infectious. The final result was that fewer men were required in the stores and most articles would now be supplied on demand. He then tackled the running sheds and instituted the same system there.

In all this reorganization, Riddles regards his crowning triumph as an instruction to paint all the store bins in an eau-de-nil shade. The running sheds protested that in the dirty surroundings it would be impossible to keep bins looking green, and particularly light green. Riddles insisted, and achieved the immediate result that he expected: storesmen and storeswomen acquired dusting brushes and a pride in keeping the bins clean, which in turn (and this was the object of the instruction) led to efficiency reaching an unprecedented level. (Riddles had brought this idea from St Rollox, where he had had all the machines in the machine shop painted, with the result that they were kept really clean. This idea of painting, which he had started, eventually spread throughout British Railways, and when he visited Derby in 1969 he found that even the floors had been painted.)

When Fairburn became CME after Stanier's retirement he fixed his headquarters at Derby. He was, as already stated, essentially an electrical engineer, with little knowledge of steam. One of his strangest acts, perhaps because of this lack of knowledge, was to build in the carriage shops at Derby a full size 2–6–2 tank engine, complete down to the last detail, but constructed entirely in wood. He never seems to have explained the reason for this peculiar project, except that it was for inspection and comment by shed staffs. But it does not appear that it ever served any useful purpose. and when Ivatt became CME he broke it up.

The only new steam locomotive design produced during Fairburn's time was a modernized version of Stanier's 2–6–4 tank engine. But his chief claim to fame was the development of the diesel-electric shunter. This excellent engine was adopted by British Railways and multiplied till 1,400 of them were at work all over Great Britain. The LMS had at first got interested in diesel shunters during the depression of 1931, and between 1932 and 1934 eleven were ordered. One of them, with electric drive, was built by English Electric, and it was from this firm that Fairburn came to the LMS as Electrical Engineer. As such, he would only consider electric drive, and so the diesel-electric shunter was selected for all future development. In 1935 20 further diesel-electric shunters were ordered, of which 10 came from English Electric and 10 from Armstrong Whitworth. The former were the more satisfactory, and another 40 were ordered with the design modified and a jackshaft drive. In a later order, the jackshaft disappeared and the engines had six-coupled wheels and two nose-suspended motors. Twenty of these went into service in 1944, and the last six were of the design which became standard for the LMS and British Railways.

During 1945 there were a number of bent side rods on the rebuilt Royal Scots. Fairburn became extremely worried about this, though Ivatt explained that it was entirely due to bad driving. The rebuilt engines, having more power, were inclined to slip. Some drivers of the unrebuilt engines had been in the bad habit of applying sand before shutting off steam, and if, as often happened, one wheel received sand before the others there was a tendency to slip. With the rebuilt engines this became more than a tendency. When this bad habit was eradicated the trouble ceased.

After Riddles' return to the LMS, which Ivatt says worried him, Fairburn decided to move back to Euston. The move took place just after the end of the War, but he died suddenly in hospital in October 1945. Immediately there was speculation about his successor. Riddles thought that it might be him, and says that he was surprisingly lacking in enthusiasm. He was happy in the stores and comfortably settled in his domestic life, and did not want another upheaval. Nevertheless, for a locomotive engineer it was the ultimate goal, if for the vast majority unobtainable. When in January 1946 it was announced that Ivatt, who had been carrying on as acting CME, had been selected, Riddles' pride received a severe shock. He accordingly asked to see the President of the LMS, Sir William Wood, a man for whom he had a great admiration. Wood was a dedicated railwayman with an astounding grasp of railway economics and an almost uncanny knowledge of every railway activity from the rival technical merits of locomotives to the business of running ships. 'He was', says Riddles, 'a man of few words, which was perhaps as well, for he never opened lips which were always firmly gripping a cigarette, and it was extremely difficult to understand what he was saying. But a more honest and conscientious man I have yet to meet.' The interview was brief. Riddles said that he had come to see Sir William about Ivatt's appointment to CME. He added that he had not the slightest doubt that he would do the job well, but said that he must point out that he was senior to him, being a Chief Officer already, and that with his knowledge and past record he did feel that he should have been considered more favourably. He finished, 'But, Sir William, if you tell me that you and the Board are satisfied that Ivatt is in your opinion more fitted to the job, I will accept that and will help him all I can'. They were standing up and Sir William looked Riddles straight in the eye. The cigarette wobbled. 'Yes, we did,' he muttered. 'Thank you, Sir, I accept that.' And Riddles retired from the room.

Five days later Sir William Wood sent for Riddles. The cigarette wobbled again at him, as a mutter came out: 'The Board, on my recommendation, have decided to appoint you Vice-President in place of Hartley, who is to retire.' Wood had known at the previous interview that Riddles was destined to be the man to whom Ivatt would be responsible!

A voice from the past was one of the first to congratulate him. On April 19, 1946, Hewitt Beames, now Chairman of the Cheshire County Council, wrote, 'I hear that you have been elevated to the highly rarefied atmosphere in which only Vice-Presidents can breathe in freedom. My most hearty congratulations. It is a long way from Clerk of Works in charge of the re-construction of Crewe Works to Vice-President of the LMS'. It was indeed; and perhaps Hewitt Beames deserves credit for being the first to spot the potentialities in the fitter from Rugby.

CHAPTER XII

Developments in Railway Traction

The appointment of Riddles to one of the pinnacles of railway service is perhaps a suitable juncture to discuss the progress of railway motive power, other than the conventional steam with which he had been primarily concerned. As Vice-President for Engineering he had to take decisions on trials with main line diesel power on the LMS, and later, as Member for Mechanical and Electrical Engineering on the Railway Executive, he had to select the motive power for British Railways and was responsible for the first trials of 50-cycle 25 kV electric traction in Great Britain.

There are three main types of railway traction to be considered—diesel, electric, and compound steam as designed by A. Chapelon for the French Railways.

Diesel

One of the most remarkable occurrences in railway history is the speed with which diesel traction replaced steam on most of the non-electrified lines of the world. Diesel shunters had, as stated in the last chapter, been introduced on the LMS before the Second World War and had been accepted as generally superior to steam locomotives for this type of work. Diesel powered trains of various types had appeared on fast passenger services, particularly in Germany and the United States of America, before the outbreak of war. In the former there had been the noteworthy 'Flying Hamburger' and other similar trains running very fast inter-city services from 1932 onwards. (The 'Flying Hamburger', in fact, had led the LNER to enquire into the possibility of a train of this type providing a high speed service between London and Newcastle. However, subsequent research had shown that steam could provide just as fast a service and convey more passengers.) In the United States, the Chicago, Burlington and Quincy Railroad introduced their very fast Zephyr series of diesel trains from 1934. More modestly, the Great Western Railway, in the same year, had started running diesel railcars for passenger and parcel traffic. But all these were subsidiary to steam because they were restricted to special type of services and were not operated by locomotives. Until main-line diesel locomotives were available to haul freight trains and passenger trains of variable make-up and length, diesel traction could not replace steam in general operation.

Diesel locomotives had, it is true, been built at intervals over many years, but without any marked impact on railway operation. Their first successful appearance was in the United States in 1935 when the Electro-Motive Company of General Motors produced two locomotives, which, coupled in multiple unit control developed 3,600 hp equal, the makers considered, to the average large American steam locomotive. The performance of this diesel pair was certainly impressive. They hauled a ten-coach passenger train weighing 757 tons a distance of 1,114 miles, without change, from Jersey City to St Louis. They then waited two hours before hauling another passenger train, weighing 808 tons, over the 284 miles to Chicago. As a result of these runs the Electro-Motive Company calculated that their twin locomotives could haul a train of from 12 to 14 coaches at a cost from 40 to 60 per cent less than that of a steam locomotive of equivalent power.

The next important event after this trial was the sale to the Baltimore & Ohio Railroad, of a 1,800 hp locomotive, similar to the above units, which was placed in service in 1935. The next year the Santa Fé Railroad brought two similar units and operated them in multiple as a 3,600 hp locomotive. In 1937 they were working the new 'Super Chief' train between Chicago and Los Angeles in the record scheduled time of 39¾ hours—a 2,227 mile run without change of locomotives.

These events threw a 'spot-light' on diesel performance with long distance expresses; but main line diesel traction was still regarded as suitable only for a special class of high-speed passenger train. In 1937 Electro-Motive, now a Division of General Motors, began selling a 1,800 hp passenger locomotive, designated E-1, which was a considerable advance on previous models. It had a wheel arrangement of A1A–A1A, and could be bought either as a 'cab' unit or a 'booster' unit—it being intended that the two should be coupled in multiple. Both the Baltimore & Ohio and the Santa Fé Railroads purchased the E–1 for hauling long-distance passenger trains.

In 1938 Electro-Motive produced an improved version of the E–1 in the E–6 2,000 hp locomotive. It became the first main line diesel locomotive to be mass-produced and it was designed for three-unit operation, that is to say, a booster unit between two cab units, to form a 6,000 hp locomotive. The Seaboard Airline used it to haul its 'Orange Blossom Special' between Washington and Miami with such success that a competing line cancelled its order for 4–8–4 steam locomotives and bought E–6s. Many other railways followed suit.

Riddles rode on an E–6 locomotive hauling the 'Orange Blossom Special' from Washington to Palm Beach in March 1939. He says says that the ease with which the engine handled the train was impressive but that the trip was very dull. The driver had only to observe signals and speed restrictions, and push the controller over as necessary. Even when the mechanic who rode in the 'engine room' switched an engine out it made no difference to the performance of the locomotive. The three units, each with two 1,000 hp engines, totalled 210 feet in length, and Riddles had a mental vision of this 210 feet of locomotive alongside one of the restricted British terminal platforms.

So far diesel locomotives, apart from shunters, had been built only for passenger service, and were not yet therefore in a position to replace steam engines. The latter were, indeed, still being built in large numbers. Many railway companies doubted the ability of diesel locomotives to stand up to the rough duty inseparable from the haulage of heavy freight trains. In any case, the 1,000 hp engines with which the E–6 locomotives were equipped were hardly powerful enough for the haulage of American freight trains without the complexity of multiple engines and generators. But in 1939 there came the development which made the diesel conquest of railways possible. Electro-Motive produced a 1,350 hp engine and installed one in each unit of a four-unit locomotive, No. 103, which thus developed 5,400 hp. It could be divided, if required, to operate as two 2,700 hp locomotives. No. 103 produced a starting tractive effort of 220,000 lbs., about twice that of the biggest steam locomotives in normal service. It was essentially a freight engine and was geared for a maximum speed of 75 mph. For over a year it ran tests on 20 different railways, covering 83,764 miles in temperatures varying from −40 degrees Fahrenheit to 115 degrees Fahrenheit and at altitudes from sea level to 10,240 feet. No delays were attributable to the engine and it put up some phenomenal performances. In California, for instance, the heavy 1 in 40 gradient up to the Tehachapi Loop took the biggest articulated steam locomotives 2 hours 15 minutes with a load of 1,350 tons. No. 103, with 1,800 tons, did it in 1½ hours. Over the easy gradients through Ohio into Pennsylvania, No. 103 pulled 5,000 tons as compared with 2,800 tons hauled by the normal steam engine operating on the same schedule. Finally, the costs for the diesel's whole tour were stated to be less than half those incurred by steam. These results were sufficiently impressive for thirteen of the twenty railways over which the diesel had run to order similar locomotives, which were called Class FT.

In Europe the Second World War had now started. In December 1941 the United States War Production Board banned the construction of passenger locomotives for the duration of the war. Production of main-line (or 'line service') freight diesels was confined to their biggest builder, Electro-Motive. The freight diesels were now in great demand and production of steam engines declined rapidly: 326 were built in 1944, 115 in 1946, 57 in 1949, and 12 in 1950. By 1956 steam had been practically eliminated from the main United States railways.

The rapidity of this switch in motive power and the ruthless scrapping of masses of modern steam engines is still something of a puzzle, even though it has been repeated subsequently in numerous other countries, including the United Kingdom. Once it was agreed that dieselization was desirable it could be, and was, argued that it was uneconomic to operate the two types of traction at the same time, and steam should be got rid of as soon as possible. As to its being desirable, the diesel enthusiasts claimed that, though its economic life of not more than fifteen years was about half that of a steam locomotive, during that life a diesel locomotive produced about three times the amount of work and that, with no fire to clean and no boiler to wash out, it was capable of giving six and a half days of service out of seven. (But this calculation took no account of days out of service due to breakdown of the diesel's more complex mechanism.) Nevertheless, for long trips over those great areas of the United States where water was short the diesel did offer another advantage over the steam engine, for the latter had to haul a lot of extra water which reduced the pay load considerably.

Some very interesting trials were carried out on the New York Central Railroad which showed that a modern steam locomotive was only slightly inferior to a diesel, given equal conditions of maintenance. It has been argued that these trials were of very limited duration, and that had they been extended over several years the diesel would have shown itself to be greatly superior. But this is a rather hypothetical argument, and it does seem that in most cases the diesel was compared with steam locomotives which could not really be considered of modern design.

Diesel locomotive construction in the United States was probably given a tremendous boost by the requirements of war. Production was limited and allocation restricted to railways with either experience in operating diesels or a particular need for them; but perhaps the thwarted demand for this new power, which had given such spectacular results just before the War, increased the demand for it. It is conceivable, though this is speculation, that at the end of the War, there was pressure to keep the diesel production going, and that this pressure spread overseas with attractive terms to replace steam stock by diesels. But even if these speculations should be valid, it remains a puzzle that railway administrators should have been in such a hurry to replace their well-tried equipment by this glamorous siren, which cost far more, which was far more complex, and which was so new that there was little, or no evidence as to the length of its useful life or as to whether costs rose steeply with advancing age.

Electric Traction

Probably most railway engineers would agree that electricity provides the ideal system of traction. Because it draws its power from a central source, an electric locomotive or railcar can, like a steam engine, develop for a short time an extra effort to meet temporarily increased demands—unlike a diesel unit which cannot exceed its designed horse power. It is true, of course, that most diesels are electric locomotives, but they have to carry their prime mover about with them, and hence the power of the latter is limited to the size which can be fitted into the locomotive. Although when supplies are drawn from conductors the power of a locomotive is limited to the capacity of its motors, these can be made of such a size that heavy or exceptional overloads can be accepted.

The idea of supplying power from a central source is, of course, almost as old as railways. Its advantages were realized by the engineers who built the rope-operated mineral lines, with winding engines every few miles. The rope failed, because it was too inflexible; and so did the 'rope' of air, the atmospheric railway, for the same reason and because of technical difficulties. It was only when the 'rope' was made of electricity that operation of trains from a central source became really feasible.

But rope or cable haulage remained (and it is still not extinct) to work trains where the steam locomotive was unsuitable. In England it was proposed for the City & South London, the first of the tube railways, but history was made when the Company in 1890 decided to adopt electric traction instead, and so introduced electricity to Great Britain for normal railway operation.

Although in these early days there were the first movements of main line electric traction, most electrified railways were either urban or suburban. In England, indeed, it was the urban systems of electric tramways which, by their competition, stimulated the electrification of suburban railway lines. Electric traction was particularly suited to suburban railways because the intensive train service could be expected to repay the high capital cost of construction and installation. It was also suited to the operation of mountain railways where steep gradients demanded power beyond the normal capacity of steam, and for working trains through long tunnels where smoke from a preceding train could blind and choke the crew of one following.

Switzerland, a mountainous country with long railway tunnels, abundant water power, and no natural resources of coal or oil, was ideally suited for electrifying railways. Indeed the Swiss railways were already thinking of electrification at the start of the century for these very reasons. The Gotthard tunnel, the first of the big tunnels through the Alps, was, when it was opened, operated by steam locomotives, but smoke soon became a problem. The Simplon, with gradients rising towards the centre, was likely to be far worse because locomotives would have to be fired in each direction of running. The Simplon Railway, opened in 1906, was therefore electrified from the start. In 1910 the Lötschberg tunnel was opened by the Berne-Lötschberg-Simplon Railway, and was also electrified, but by single-phase a.c., as compared with the three-phase system adopted by the Simplon. These installations heralded the complete electrification of the Swiss Railways, most of which was carried out during the ten years after the end of the First World War. Stemming from this early start, Swiss design of electric locomotives has been outstanding, and the production in 1965 of an 80-ton locomotive, mounted on two four-wheel bogies and developing 6,240 hp emphasizes the vast superiority of the electric over the diesel locomotive.

Switzerland, for the above reasons, is rather a special case, and France provides probably the best example of a country where all major main lines have been electrified without there being any such particular reasons as mountainous terrain, long tunnels, or intensive service. It is also the country in which the most important development in electric traction in recent years was initiated.

The first projects for electrification on the Midi Railway originated in 1902 in connection with a metre gauge line in the Pyrenees. In considering wider electrification projects, the Midi decided in 1910 to try and ascertain the best methods of overhead electrification and the most suitable locomotives by a series of trials. As a result of these trials, there was by 1914 quite an extensive electric mileage at 12 kV $16\frac{2}{3}$ cycles a.c. in the neighbourhood of the Pyrenees. The outbreak of war prevented further development.

During the War there had been periods when it had been extremely difficult to provide fuel for steam engines, because the collieries in the North of France were in enemy hands and German submarine blockade made it extremely difficult to get coal from England. To prevent such a situation arising again, it was decided to institute a vast programme of electrification on the PO, Midi, and PLM Railways, in whose territory there were abundant reserves of hydraulic energy from the installations in the Alps, the Massif Central, and the Pyrenees. There were, indeed, coal mines in the Massif Central and the Midi, but little of the coal that they produced was suitable for locomotives.

In 1917, following a mission to the United States by French engineers, it was decided to electrify the main lines of the three systems at 1,500-volts d.c. This type of supply was selected on account of the results obtained in America. By 1927 the Midi main line from Bordeaux to Irun on the Spanish frontier was electrified and the earlier Midi electric sections had been converted to the new standard system. On the neighbouring PO (with which the Midi was amalgamated on January 1, 1934) the line from Paris to Vierzon was electrified on December 22, 1926. Further electrification southward into the Massif Central was postponed, as traffic had fallen off, and the next line to be tackled was that from Orléans (on the Paris-Vierzon stretch) to Tours, and this was completed in 1933. Electrification south of Vierzon was soon continued and was completed to Brive in May 1935. The important link between Tours and Bordeaux was now approved, but this was not opened until March 1939, after the incorporation of all French Railways in the SNCF. This completed one of the most important main lines in Europe, from Paris to the Spanish frontier; and the world-famous 'Sud Express' became electrically hauled over the whole of the some 500 miles of this route.

The important development mentioned above was 50-cycle a.c. traction. The French had not originated it, but it was they who first applied it in a modern form to the electrification of main lines. The idea was, in fact, pretty old. Between 1915 and 1920 a Hungarian engineer, Koloman Kando, worked out a system of using single phase a.c., taking the 50 c/s supply directly from the national grid system at 16 kV, and applying it to a phase converter locomotive developed by the firm of Ganz & Co. of which Kando was Chief Engineer. On this the single phase was converted to three-phase. The locomotive was tested on a special line near Budapest for many years, and its success led to a 50 c/s electrification scheme in 1933 between Budapest and the Austrian frontier, at Hegyeshalom (119 miles).

The system was next taken up by Germany and the 48-mile Höllenthal Railway from the Rhine to the Black Forest was made into a test route. This line was mainly single track with gradients of 1 in 18. The supply was at 20 kV and there were four experimental locomotives all of different designs and from different manufacturers. The line was opened for operation in 1936. At the end of the Second World War the Höllenthal Railway was in the French zone of occupied Germany, and French engineers, who took over the running of it, were very impressed with the potentialities. As a result of their reports the SNCF decided to electrify on the same system the 55-mile stretch of track between Aix-le-Bains and La Roche-sur-Foron on the steeply graded Geneva-Chamonix line. There was only one sub-station, at Annecy. The line is single track with several tunnels and gradients up to 1 in 50. Test running, starting on October 6, 1950, was so impressive that the SNCF decided to electrify the line between Thionville and Valenciennes at 50 c/s a.c. but with the higher tension of 25 kV., and this was authorized in 1952. This line is one of the most important freight routes in Europe and carries a very heavy traffic. Operating results confirmed the high opinion which the French had formed of the 50 c/s system, and it was decided that it would be used for all future electrification. In pursuance of this policy, the main line of the old Nord Railway between Paris and Lille was so electrified, and this became the 'show-piece' for the new generation of French electric trains.

The advantages of the new system were manifest: current could be taken direct from the standard industrial supply; owing to the high tension, only light conductors were necessary, with the result that only light structures were required; and with the low voltage drop (due to the high tension) few sub-stations were needed.

Chapelon Steam

It is worth giving a brief account of the remarkable steam locomotives designed by M. André Chapelon, firstly because they had a considerable influence on later British steam locomotive design, and secondly because the question has sometimes been asked as to why similar locomotives could not have been built for British Railways.

Early in the twentieth century the Paris-Orléans Railway decided that more powerful engines than the existing Atlantics and 4–6–0s were needed to haul the increasingly heavy traffic over the main line to Bordeaux and the mountainous inland route to Toulouse respectively. After considering various projects, they directed that two classes of Pacific engines should be designed, one with 6 feet 4¾ inches coupled wheels for the easier routes and the other with 6 feet ¾ inch wheels for the more heavily graded lines. These two types were known as the 3500 and 4500 classes, respectively. The latter appeared first, in 1907, whilst the former began to come out in 1909; they were thus roughly contemporary with the Great Western Railway Pacific *The Great Bear*. They were four-cylinder compounds on the du Bousquet de Glehn system, like their Atlantic and 4–6–0 predecessors, with outside high pressure and inside low pressure cylinders and independent Walschaerts valve gear. The 4500 class were the first of the Pacific type in Europe.

After the First World War the PO company wished to re-establish its express services at the same speeds as in 1914, but with heavier trains. This was beyond the capacity of the existing Pacifics. The obvious solution would have been to build new and more powerful engines; but it had already been decided that the PO main lines should be electrified. The Company therefore decided to meet the situation temporarily by rebuilding existing stock. And so electrification, paradoxically, resulted in the appearance of some of the most remarkable steam locomotives ever to have been built.

In 1926 a brilliant young engineer, M. André Chapelon, had carried out tests on the exhausts of the 4500 class Pacifics of both the saturated and superheated varieties. These tests demonstrated that the steam passages from regulator to exhaust were far too restricted. They also showed the manifest superiority of the Finnish 'Kylala' blast pipe.

M. Maurice Lacoin, Engineer in Chief of Material and Traction, directed the Material Branch to find means of improving the 3500 class Pacifics. M. Billet, Chief Engineer of Material, charged M. Chapelon with the task of examining the problem. In the meantime, the fitting of trick valves to No. 3584 having proved unsuccessful, it had been decided to equip Nos. 3579 and 3565 (later changed to 3566) with Lentz poppet valves. Chapelon proposed a far more drastic rebuilding of No. 3566, which would include doubling the cross-section of the steam passages between regulator and exhaust, doubling the degree of superheat, and fitting his own modification of the Kylala exhaust (the Kylchap). This had already been tried out on the 4500 class and had reduced the back-pressure by half, but now Chapelon proposed to cut this back pressure still further by fitting a double chimney. The whole project was approved in November 1926, at the same time as preparations were being made to carry out trials with No. 3579 before it went into Tours Works to be fitted with the poppet valves proposed by Messrs Paxman of London, licensees of the Lentz patent.

No. 3566 included also a Nicholson thermic syphon to improve the circulation of the water, steam chests of large volume, built-up crank axle, mechanical greasing to the cylinders and axle boxes, an ACFI feed water heater, and Lentz poppet valves actuated by the existing Walschaerts valve gear. The engine was ready and ran its first trial on November 19, 1929. To say that the results were revolutionary as compared with the unrebuilt engines is almost an understatement. The engine made trial runs not only on the PO but also on the Est, and was so outstanding in its performance that it was decided to build ten more engines—Nos. 3501–3520 of 1910—which were still saturated. This was done in the Tours Works in 1931, and the whole twenty-one rebuilt engines were re-numbered 3701–3721. They entered service in the summer of 1932 on the express trains and heavy 'rapides' on the non-electrified sections between Orléans and Bordeaux and between Tours and Nantes, putting up sensational performances. The Nord Railway, in search of new express power, became interested. Trials took place on that system in 1932 with a Chapelon Pacific, a PLM C class 4–8–2, an Est 4–8–2, and a Nord Pacific. As a result of these trials the Nord ordered twenty of the Chapelon Pacifics, which were rebuilt at Tours in 1933–4. The PO also ordered another ten for its own needs, in which Chapelon incorporated still further improvements. In 1934 the Est ordered twenty-three engines, which were rebuilt at Tours in 1935.

Meanwhile the line to Toulouse was in difficulties over motive power and M. Epinay (who had succeeded M. de Boysson, who had in turn succeeded M. Lacoin) agreed to Chapelon's suggestion that he should rebuild the 4500 class Pacifics in a similar fashion to the 3500 class, but converting them into 4–8–0s. This would entail the substitution of a narrow deep firebox for the wide one. The first engine, No. 4521, was completed in August 1932 and showed itself capable of a continuous drawbar horsepower of 3,000 at 60 mph. Between 1933 and 1934 eleven more were rebuilt at Tours, and the batch of twelve were renumbered 4701–4712. In 1940 there were twenty-five more with strengthened frames, bigger L.P. cylinders, and cleaner lines. They proved to be capable, not only of doing the job for which they were designed, but of hauling the fastest trains on the Bordeaux line. They were, indeed, the most powerful express passenger engines in Europe.

British locomotive engineers had followed the great work of Chapelon with more than ordinary interest, and they all regarded him as outstanding in the profession. Stanier and Gresley were greatly impressed with Chapelon's theories on sizes of steam passages and Stanier did a great deal of development on this with his Chief Draughtsman. The Kylchap exhaust, the ACFI feed water heater, the Lentz valve gear, and the Nicholson thermic syphon, were also tried out on British locomotives, but without any convincing improvement over modern locomotives without them. The thermic syphon had proved difficult to maintain, and Stanier asked Riddles to ask George Emerson, Chief of Motive Power on the Delaware & Hudson Railroad, privately, what he thought of this equipment. Emerson pulled a booklet out of a drawer and tossed it accross to Riddles. 'That's what I think', he said. The booklet described the complications experienced with the Nicholson thermic syphon and the methods of repairing it. This decided Stanier not to proceed with it.

M. Chapelon eventually became Engineer in Chief of the SNCF and many locomotives constructed by the other French railways were rebuilt to his designs. It is not within the scope of this book to give any detailed description of his work, but mention must be made of two engines. The first was his experimental conversion of a PO 2–10–0, which came out from the Tours Works in 1940 as a six-cylinder compound 2–12–0. By that time the Germans had broken through the Allied armies and were advancing rapidly south. Chapelon's precious engine was despatched south in front of them from Tours to Brive, hauling a 1,200-ton freight train and not dropping below 25 mph over the

1 in 100 gradients. The engine was particularly noteworthy for incorporating an additional superheater between the two high pressure and four low pressure cylinders. After this run it was hidden away and not brought out for testing until 1946. It then performed excellently on both freight and express passenger trains, in spite of its coupled wheels of only 4 feet 7 inches diameter (thus supporting Riddles' contention that with modern designs the diameter of the driving wheels is of no material importance). The second engine was a conversion of a three-cylinder simple Etat 4–8–2 of 1932, which Chapelon rebuilt into a three-cylinder compound 4–8–4 in 1946. This remarkably successful engine was the most powerful steam locomotive ever to be operated outside North America. In 1942 this engine, No. 242A1, hauled a 20-coach train weighing 810 tons from Paris to Le Mans on the same schedule as the lighter and electrically hauled express trains. (Mr. G. W. Carpenter of the *Railway Gazette* says that the engine developed 5,000–5,500 ihp for lengthy periods during tests on the Paris-Lyons line; and the 202 electric locomotives building for operation on this line were redesigned, with the one hour rating raised from 3,700 to 4,880 hp, as a result of the performance of No. 242A1). The engine was scrapped after a short life in 1960, but the suitability of the Sauvage-Smith system of compounding had been proved and Chapelon intended to adopt this for his new designs.

It is interesting to see, indeed, how Chapelon envisaged the future of steam in France. When the construction of steam locomotives was halted on French railways, Chapelon was working on four new designs of three-cylinder compound locomotives, all having basically the same boiler with 320 lbs. pressure (though of different lengths) and the same grate area of 64·6 square feet. For express passenger service there was a 4–6–4 with 7 feet 3 inches coupled wheels and poppet valves which was intended to run at a maximum speed of 125 mph. The other three types had piston valves and comprised a 4–8–4 for heavy express passenger trains, a 2–8–4 for mixed traffic, and a 2–10–4 for heavy freight. These last were required urgently by the operating department and the cylinders had actually been cast.

However, Riddles points out that these magnificent Chapelon machines could never have been used in Great Britain for two reasons. Firstly, the restrictions of the British loading gauge did not permit the use of powerful compound locomotives. Secondly, the big French compounds demanded very specialized knowledge for their driving and maintenance. French drivers were specially trained engineers, belonging to a skilled grade to which the average fireman did not aspire to reach. British and American steam drivers, for example, were not engineers (in spite of the name applied to the latter) and could not have undertaken the duties of fitters on French engines that were expected of French drivers (which is perhaps another reason why Churchward never copied the French Atlantics which he tried on the Great Western). Chapelon provides an outstanding example of Riddles' contention that all successful steam locomotive development builds on the practice of the past. All Chapelon's engines were rebuilds of existing type and his own completely new engines, if he had been permitted to build them, would have embodied the well-tried methods adopted in the rebuilt engines. The failures have been the completely new ventures, such as in recent times were Fowler's high pressure engine *Fury*, Gresley's water-tube boiler compound engine, Stanier's *Turbomotive*, and Bulleid's *Leader*.

The above outline of three types of locomotive power gives something of the background against which Riddles had to make decisions, firstly as Vice-President, but much more so as member of the Railway Executive. By 1946 it was clear that the steam locomotive was doomed in America; in France, whilst Chapelon's brilliant engines were holding their own on many lines, steam was playing an increasingly subsidiary role to electric traction (though 50-cycle electrification had not yet appeared); and in Great Britain the steam engine was still supreme, except for passenger electrification on suburban railways.

CHAPTER XIII

Vice-President, LMS

As a Vice-President, Riddles moved into a sphere which was far removed from any of the appointments that he had previously held. He was no longer responsible for day-to-day working, or for initiating projects, such as were the concern of a departmental head. Instead he was concerned with policy, direction, and approval. The system of President and Vice-Presidents was, amongst British railway companies, peculiar to the LMS and, under the guidance of Lord Stamp, Lord Roydon, and Sir William Wood, it had become so successful that it may well have been the finest higher railway organization in the world. Any scheme proposed by the head of a department was scrutinized by the appropriate Vice-President, and it was not approved unless it was clearly shown to be both necessary and justified financially. In fact Vice-Presidents approved very few proposals unless the departmental head could prove that there were worthwhile financial profits attached to them. Furthermore, even if a project were approved it was later 'back-checked' by a special body of accountants to ascertain how far the actual results agreed with the forecast. Any major scheme was subjected to this procedure, including new machinery, locomotives, rolling stock, buildings, operating lay-outs, etc. If a Vice-President approved a scheme that had been laid before him, he discussed it with the President and other Vice-Presidents; and if they concurred, it was submitted to the directors for their authorization.

As Vice-President for Engineering, Riddles had to discuss schemes with the Engineer, the Chief Mechanical Engineer, the Signal Engineer, and the Stores Superintendent. But he got on well with his officers, and knew all their difficulties. Once they had explained their problems to him, he supported them both at the meetings of Presidents and Vice-Presidents and subsequently at the board meetings of directors. But it was never his practice to await the problems in his office; he paid frequent visits to the various works with the CME and to 'line sites' with the Chief Engineer. One of his more pleasant and lighter duties was to represent the Company at the naming of engines and other ceremonial occasions and official functions. The Research Department, set up by Sir Harold Hartley, also became Riddles' responsibility, and he says that in respect of this organization he was in the classic situation of poacher turned into gamekeeper. He had frequently criticized it in the past, but, in his heart, had always realized the value of having a department with the time and facilities to undertake investigation into failures of equipment and to explore the possibilities in new materials. He tried to get his officers to appreciate this and to make as much use as possible of the Research Department to help them in their problems. It was, he says, a very valuable asset, and much of the credit was due to Sir Harold Hartley for pressing its development.

Riddles' relations with Ivatt were particularly close, though their relative positions were reversed as compared with the days when Riddles had been Ivatt's assistant at Derby. Ivatt produced two new small class 2 engines before the end of 1946, a 2–6–0 tender and a 2–6–2 tank, both of which replaced small Midland-type 0–6–0 tender and tank engines respectively. Next, in response to a request for more of the standard class 4 0–6–0 freight engines of Midland design, he responded with another new type, a class 4 2–6–0, for he had decided that the 0–6–0 was an obsolete wheel arrangement. All these engines had outside cylinders, as compared with the inside cylinders of those they replaced.

Two more Pacifics were built in 1947 with some improvements. One was to be named *City of Salford*. The name to be selected for the other was being considered by Riddles, Ivatt, and Bond. Bond suggested 'Stanier', upon which Riddles exclaimed that it was a damned good idea and that he wished he had thought of it himself. And so No. 6256 became *Sir William Stanier, FRS*, one of the nameplates of which, as stated in Chapter VI, adorns Riddles' workshop.

But Ivatt's chief claim to fame is that he produced the first passenger diesel locomotive to run in Great Britain. He had always had a great interest in internal combustion engines, Riddles says, from the time when he had served in the Royal Army Service

Corps in the First World War, and he knew a great deal about them. He had first become interested in the possibility of a diesel-electric express passenger locomotive in 1945, but Fairburn did not respond to his suggestion that it might be worthwhile building one. When he became Acting CME he had more thoughts about this project and had mentioned it to Sir William Wood, just before Riddles was appointed Vice-President. Riddles was subsequently able to support him and get the necessary financial authority from the Board. A very large sum of money was involved in the construction of one twin-locomotive, but Riddles says that the LMS was always ready to consider a possibly worthwhile project. But in spite of the large sum which had been authorized, Ivatt's estimate was unfortunately far below the real cost, and Riddles had to ask for more money long before the locomotive was completed.

The first of the twin locomotives, No. 10000, was driven by Ivatt out of the Derby shops on December 8, 1947, though it was not completed until after Nationalization on January 1, 1948; but Ivatt had had the floor plates made with the letters LMS cast in! The twin, No. 10001, came out a little later. Bulleid of the Southern, who also wanted to be 'in' on diesel construction, followed with three more diesel-electric express locomotives, so that British Railways eventually inherited five.

It is worth glancing ahead for a moment to see how these five precursors of a traction system, which was eventually to sweep steam locomotives out of Great Britain, fared in the early days of British Railways; particularly as they were of designs inherited from the old railway companies. Riddles says that the initial difficulty in having these locomotives properly tested was that the operating people disliked them, and either could not or would not find suitable paths which would permit of their maximum use. Part of the operating objection was that they did not fit in with the 'link' system. (Drivers were grouped in 'links' according to length of service, ability, etc.) 'Top Link' drivers shared the top jobs in rotation, which meant that, with the diesels being used on the most important expresses, they might drive a diesel one day and then exclusively steam engines for the next week or so. But unless all of them were thoroughly trained in diesel operation, much trouble could result. For instance, there was an occasion when hauling the 'Night Scot' that the two diesels, coupled together, stuck on the Camden bank. A relief engine was sent for and the fireman of this, being interested in diesels, climbed in and asked what the trouble was. 'B—— if I know', said the driver. The fireman looked round, pushed the overload release button, and said, 'Now, start', And it did. The diesel had been worked too hard up the bank.

It was clear to Riddles that the diesels were not getting the best use and he arranged for all five to be allotted to the Southern Region, where, having a much smaller proportion of steam locomotives, they were anxious to try out this new power. The Southern diagrammed the diesels so that a maximum mileage could be obtained from them every day. On the whole the results were satisfactory, although the locomotives were by no means free from 'teething troubles'; but with so many new and untried devices, some were almost bound to go wrong. Ivatt, says Riddles, was undoubtedly the pioneer in British main-line diesel locomotives. After his retirement he was consultant to the Brush company, which has been a prominent builder of main-line diesel locomotives now running on British Railways. It was largely Ivatt's knowledge which was responsible for Brush's early success.

There was a change in the LMS locomotive livery in 1946. The Midland red of the express passenger locomotives was replaced by a glossy black lined out with maroon bands edged with straw yellow. It is said that Crewe adopted the new livery with enthusiasm, but that no such interest was displayed at Derby!

When Riddles became Vice-President the shadow of nationalization was already hanging over the four big railway companies. Most officers on the LMS felt very sad at the approaching end of a great company which, after the early years of disunity had developed through so much effort into an efficient and profitable railway. The future seemed bleak, for not only would they no longer belong to a railway family with a common outlook, a well-tried organization, and a familiar promotion structure, but their own personal future was unknown. To Riddles, who had had the disturbing experience of two amalgamations (first that of the LNWR with the L & YR, and secondly that which resulted in the LMS), the outlook was far from cheerful. Apart from the officers, though, he thought that the men were in favour of nationalization.

He had a suspicion that many of them believed that they would be financially better off when it came to sharing out the 'fat fees' enjoyed by the directors! (Though, as Lord Stamp had once said to shareholders who were complaining about the size of his salary, 'If I shared my salary amongst you, it would not amount to a ham sandwich apiece'.)

Before the end of 1947 the Chairman of the LMS, Sir Robert Burrows, decided to go to America and Canada to give his personal thanks to all the friends of the LMS in those countries who had helped them so much in the past. Riddles was asked to go with him, but before he left, the Minister of Transport sent for him and offered him the post of member of the Railway Executive for Mechanical and Electrical Engineering. It was a pretty frightful title, but the post was approximately that which had first been known as Locomotive Superintendent and later Chief Mechanical Engineer, and it was for the whole of British Railways. He was to have more steam locomotives under his control than any other locomotive chief before or since. He was too, though he did not know it, to be the last locomotive engineer to design steam engines for railways in Great Britain. Riddles could hardly analyse his feelings. He was very content in the position he held on the LMS, but the old ways were going, and though the task seemed quite appalling in its difficulties, he had little option but to accept.

A few days later he was on his way to America with the LMS Chairman. In New York they visited the headquarter offices of various railroad companies and their own New York office to say farewell. They then went on to Montreal where they met the Presidents of the Canadian Pacific and Canadian National Railways. The latter had kindly placed his own saloon at their disposal for a journey to Vancouver. It was a magnificent vehicle with bedrooms, showers, lounge, dining room, and observation platform. The train by which they were to travel arrived at the station with this coach marshalled at the end. The beds were ready and a meal was being prepared. Riddles was looking forward to the kind of enjoyable trip of which he had been deprived in 1939. But for the second time he was to be disappointed. As he boarded the train he was handed a cable. It read, 'Return at once. Urgent meetings being held. Your presence essential.' Resignedly and sadly, Riddles packed his bag, waved good-bye to the train, and flew home to his new job three months before the vesting day of British Railways.

It was a formidable task. An entirely new organization had to be set up, embracing great railways of vastly different traditions and ways of doing things. All had talented and dedicated men amongst their senior officers, and, as with all such, they had preconceived ideas and most of them had strong loyalties to their old companies. To make the thing work the seven men of the new Executive had three months to produce their plans. Of the seven, Riddles had perhaps the most daunting job of the lot, for under him were to come the four Chief Mechanical Engineers who had been presiding over four entirely different practices in design and manufacture. Compared with the problem of reconciling these, the problems raised by the differences between Crewe and Derby seemed comparatively trivial. But to Beames, who again sent him a congratulatory letter, it must have been a consolation after the bitterness of the past that a London and North Western man had been given the most important post in British steam locomotive history.

Above: Austerity 2–10–0 the '1000th British Built War Dept Main Line Locomotive Ferried to Europe since D-Day'

Below: The 1000th and 1001st locomotives being loaded on to a Southern Railway train ferry

By kind permission of British Railways

Above: An Austerity Class 2–10–0 hauling a freight train

Below: An Austerity Class 2–8–0 hauling a coal train near Watford
By kind permission of British Railways

Right: A cartoon, 'Dropping the Pilot *or* The Riddle of the Universe' drawn by J. P. Sayer of his Camouflage Section when Riddles left the Royal Engineer Equipment branch to return to the LMS. (The cartoon is based on the famous Punch drawing with the same title showing the Kaiser dismissing *Bismark*)

Below: Rebuilt Royal Scot Class *The Boy Scout* on a Manchester–Euston express

By kind permission of British Railways

Above: Duchess Class Pacific the *King George VI* leaving Euston

Below: Duchess Class Pacific *Duchess of Devonshire* climbing Shap
By kind permission of British Railways

CHAPTER XIV

The Railway Executive

On January 1, 1948, the LMSR, LNER, GWR, SR, and London Transport were nationalized and placed under the British Transport Commission, of which Sir Cyril (later Lord) Hurcomb was Chairman. The various activities controlled by the Transport Commission were managed by five public authorities called Executives. One of these, the Railway Executive, was responsible for the railways previously under the ownership of the four main line companies. The Railway Executive consisted of seven full time men: Sir Eustace Missenden (late General Manager Southern Railway, Chairman), General Sir William Slim, Mr R. A. Riddles (late Vice-President London, Midland & Scottish Railway), Mr W. P. Allen, Mr V. M. Barrington-Ward (late Assistant General Manager, Operating, London & North Eastern Railway), Mr D. Blee (late Chief Goods manager, Great Western Railway), and Mr J. C. L. Train (late Chief Civil Engineer, London & North Eastern Railway). All were appointed until September 30, 1952. (General Sir William Slim was to become quite unique in the annals of the Army. He had at this time retired, but he was later recalled to the active list, appointed Chief of the Imperial General Staff, and subsequently promoted Field Marshal, and as such, of course, never retired again!) In addition to these full-time members there were two part-time from outside the Railway.

On his return from America in October 1947 Riddles found that the Railway executive had already assembled and were working in a room in 55, Broadway (the well-known headquarters of London Transport) placed at their disposal by the Pullman Car Company. Initially the work consisted of long discussions as to how the nationalized railway system was to be organized. There were frequently hotly contested arguments, for there were very different opinions in many matters. Some members felt, for instance, that the old railway hierarchy should disappear, that anything savouring of a manager or chief of anything was not in keeping with the concept of a nationalized railway system. Riddles opposed vehemently the pseudo-democratic levelling of grades, insisting that status was generally more important than pay in achieving efficiency, and that a good title often made a good man. He won his point, and eventually agreement was hammered out both as to the organization in general and the detailed tasks, appointments, and titles in the various departments.

Having settled the framework, the members were now faced with the arrangement of their own specific responsibilities. Riddles had to deal with four eminent CMEs, each of whom believed firmly that his own policies, evolved from a long line of predecessors, alone pointed the way to the goal of locomotive perfection. If the job was to be done successfully, it was essential that he should persuade both them and their staffs to work with him and not against him. He had to make them see that his sole aim was to take all that was best from the design and works practice of the four Companies so that British Railways should ultimately possess the most efficient and economical motive power obtainable. He was certain that nothing in the way of revolutionary development should be attempted. Obviously, the first task was to examine all that had been done in the recent past. Then, having set up standards of design and practice as a result of this study, it would be necessary to persuade the Chief Mechanical Engineers and Chief Electrical Engineers, and their staffs, to accept these new standards and practices as the best. It was clear that, since all railways had their own specialities in the various components of the steam engine, some must be better than others. At the same time, it would have been almost, or even quite, impossible to persuade any one Company to adopt any idea that had originated in another. Nationalization, however, provided the opportunity to select the best. But it was sensitive ground and Riddles would have to be absolutely neutral. (He considered that he had become well experienced at this at the Ministry of Supply.)

The selection of his staff was important and, in spite of the necessity of appearing neutral, he felt that he must take people he knew, which meant that the majority would have to come from the LMS. From his old Company, therefore came R. C. Bond, E. S. Cox, E. Pugson, and C. Dennett (the last being his personal assistant). C. M. Cock came from the Southern as electrical engineer, later to be relieved by S. B. Warder. Bond had been in charge of both St Rollox and Crewe Works and had then become Deputy to the CME, Ivatt. Cox had an outstanding capacity for putting things together and recording (and, as Stanier, Ivatt and Riddles all found out, he was invaluable when one had to make a speech). Pugson was the most knowledgeable and practical of any carriage and wagon engineer whom Riddles had ever encountered. In terms of the number of staff and expenditure, his was to be the biggest department. He became responsible, not only for manufacture and works maintenance, but also for running. All except Cock had been brought up under the LMS system, laid down by Lord Stamp and developed by Sir William Wood, which insisted on expenditure being included as an essential item of any project. It was men who were well grounded in these principles that Riddles needed so that he would not feel obliged to check their work. Nevertheless, so anxious was he not to appear biased in favour of the LMS that he asked CMEs for any nominations for the nucleus of his staff, other than those he had chosen. However, none of them commented, for they realized his difficulties and they all gave him such help as they could.

His disbandment of the Association of Railway Locomotive Engineers caused some comment; but with the disappearance of the old companies and their separate CMEs there was really no need for its continued existence. The ARLE had been an association for exchanging ideas and proposing common standards in design, and it had met regularly for discussion. But the only thing it ever effectively did was to agree standard tyre profiles; and even these, though adopted after many months by the remaining companies, were rejected by the Great Western who insisted on deeper flanges. (A similar organization existed in America, and Riddles attended one of their sessions. The subject under discussion was a brass valve, about which, after months of debate, they had agreed the size and shape but not the metal mixture. It was eventually decided that as long as the valve bore the stamp of the Society it could be made of any mixture for brass, and honour was satisfied!)

The Railway Executive moved into 222, Marylebone Road later in October 1947 (each, says Riddles, 'grabbing what furniture he could get from his late Railway. I took all mine from Euston'), and here they settled down to work as a body.

For the various activities which came under him, Riddles appointed three Chief Officers: Bond for locomotive construction and maintenance; Pugson for carriage and wagon construction and maintenance; and Cock for electrical engineering. In addition, the Chief Officer for motive power, H. Rudgard, (also of the LMS) was jointly responsible to Riddles and to the Operating Member, Barrington-Ward.

It was now necessary to reconcile the various Regional departmental organizations, which had been inherited from the old Companies, so that they all had a similar framework. Whereas on the LMSR and GWR the Chief Mechanical Engineer had been responsible for the three activities given above, on the LNER and SR there had been a Chief Electrical Engineer. In all four Companies the CME had been responsible for both locomotives and carriages, but in a number of the larger companies before the amalgamations of 1923 the two activities had been the responsibility of separate Chiefs. Owing to the size of the carriage and wagon department, Riddles decided to separate these again in each of the regions. But, on the other hand, the increasing interdependence of mechanical and electrical engineering made it desirable to combine these two at regional level under the same head on those systems where they had previously been separate. In each region there were appointed, therefore, a mechanical and electrical engineer and a carriage and wagon engineer, responsible to Riddles through his appropriate Chief Officers.

Like all mechanical engineers in a similar position, Riddles was strongly tempted to put into practice all the ideas that he had formed during his years of railway service. He resisted the temptation, however, and stuck to his own principles that all new steps in practice, design, and organization must be built on the experiences of the past. There was a wealth of experience to be derived from each of the four companies and the main problem was how to make the best use of it. He decided to set up a series of policy committees, such as, 'Carriage Standards Committee', 'Wagon Standards Committee', 'Locomotive Testing Committee', etc. Each of these committees consisted of a chairman selected by Riddles and representatives from every region. The aim of standardization was to reduce first costs, maintenance costs, and stores costs; and engineering opinion (with the exception of a few sturdy individualists) agrees that standardization, provided that the right standards are selected, is the correct policy.

It was apparent to Riddles that the main weakness in his organization was that, unlike a normal CME, he had no chief draughtsman. He had, indeed, not one drawing office, but four for locomotives and four for carriages and wagons. Chief draughtsmen were men of long and varied experience who translated their CMEs instructions into fact and even, on occasions, told CMEs why their ideas were impracticable. Riddles got over this difficulty in a most ingenious way by establishing a sort of corporate chief draughtsman, by forming the chief draughtsmen of Derby, Doncaster, Swindon, and Brighton, into a body under the chairmanship of Cox as Executive Officer Design.

Having only a general knowledge of the operating and commercial side, Riddles obtained the services of a man who was well qualified to advise him in such matters and whom he appointed Executive Officer (Administration and Special Duties). This was G. S. Hussey, an old London & North Western man who had had a very varied experience. He had started as a traffic apprentice, had served on innumerable committees, and had finally become personal assistant to a Vice-President of the LMS. He had the invaluable asset of such charm of character that he could smooth away the friction which inevitably arose in a new organization.

The erstwhile CMEs at this time were variously engaged. Ivatt was busily occupied with his diesel locomotives and the troubles that arose with them; Bulleid was trying to make a success of his controversial 'Leader' class of steam engine and was busy as well with his double deck carriage and other imaginative projects; the amiable Peppercorn was happily turning out lots of the last LNER Pacifics; and Hawksworth watched approaching events in the comfortable knowledge of Great Western superiority.

Riddles has been strongly criticized in recent years for his insistence on adhering to steam traction. Before, therefore, discussing the steam power that he chose, it would be appropriate to consider why he chose steam at all. To get matters into proper proportion one should first look at the situation in 1948 and then jump ahead to see what steam looked like at the time this book is being written (1969). The background to three forms of motive power—diesel, electric, and Chapelon steam—has been given in Chapter XII. Practically, there is little to choose between any accepted form of railway motive power, because a like value of power in any of these forms will result in a comparable output in both loads and speeds. But economically they are not equal, and it is an extremely difficult and complex matter to determine the true cost of each. With a wealth of figures, it is hard to find a solid base of fact amidst the many shifting sands of theory; and the search is made no easier by the host of biased opinions and commercial sales pressures which help to fog the issue. Facts are, of course, what the engineer needs, because it is on facts that he bases and presents his case.

On the prices current in 1950, certain comparative costs of locomotives of different forms of power were calculated as follows:

Type	*Capital Cost*	*Starting TE lbs.*	*Cost per lb. of TE*	*1 hr. DBHP*	*Cost per DBHP*
B.R. Class 5 4-6-0-	£16,000	26,120	£0-12-3	1,200	£13-6-0
1,600 hp Diesel-Elec.	£78,200	41,400	£1-17-9	1,200	£65-0-0
2,500 hp Gas-Turbine	£138,700	33,000	£4-4-0	2,000	£69-7-0
CC Electric 1,500 V	£37,400	45,000	£0-16-8	2,120	£17-12-10

On the above basis steam comes out an easy winner with the electric locomotive second. The money can, with steam, too, be spent without exceptional capital investment at any one time. And, although the thermal efficiency of steam is low, actual fuel costs per drawbar horsepower do not rank very high in total relative costs. In addition, substantial developments were still being introduced on the mechanical side in 1951 to reduce the costs of the steam locomotive and increase its availability. But of course there are factors other than the above calculations such as are mentioned in Chapter XII.

Too often, in comparing steam locomotives with newer forms of power, the former have been some thirty years old and the latter brand new, and the true comparison has been still further clouded because the modern steam locomotive, with capacity for a performance far superior to its predecessors, was tied to schedules which had been virtually unaltered for many years. Yet these schedules were revised as a matter of course to ensure the best results from diesel and electric traction.

Like many others, Sir Cyril Hurcomb had been thinking about the possibilities of diesel and electric traction as an alternative to steam, and in April 1948 he wrote to the Chairman of the Railway Executive, Sir Eustace Missenden, saying that the technical capabilities of these were now fairly well appreciated and suggesting that a committee, not composed of engineers, should be set up to review the question of motive power on economic grounds. The Executive duly appointed a committee consisting of two operating officers, an administrative officer, and an accountant. It held its first meeting at the end of 1948 but, for various reasons, did not submit its report until 1951. Predictably the report referred to the great success of diesel traction in the United States and of electrification and diesel railcars in Europe. It noted, more debatedly, that these forms of traction had made possible a vast improvement in the speed and character of passenger traffic, in the operation of freight traffic, and in the working conditions of staff. With some caution, it recommended a pilot main-line electrification, tests of main-line diesel traction using 2,000-hp locomotives, an investigation into the possibility of introducing a fleet of diesel railcars, and a large increase in the number of diesel shunters. On steam the report was lukewarm. It considered that all the improvements on which Riddles was engaged were invaluable, but that they were likely to be only in matters of detail and there was no evidence of any advance in design that would overcome the inherent limitations of the steam locomotive for railway operation.

As a result of this report a working party was set up to work on the scope for lightweight diesel trains. In March 1952 it presented a report recommending areas which were considered suitable for the operation of such trains. This was accepted and plans to implement it were put in hand. An increase in the number of diesel shunters had already been proposed before the report was completed. Main-line diesel traction was a different matter; for Riddles was strongly opposed to it. He wanted eventual electrification of main lines, and he could see no reason for introducing diesels as an intermediate step—a step, moreover, which would be so expensive that it could well result in electrification being financially impossible for many years. The justification for electrifying the railways was not only its greater efficiency and cleanliness, but, just as Switzerland had no oil or coal but plenty of water power, so Great Britain had neither water power nor oil but plenty of coal; and, as in Switzerland, the operation of diesels would depend on imported fuel. There was another, and important, factor; there was no demand for diesels at this time from the operators—in fact they did not want them. But any major electrification scheme was temporarily deferred by a Government White Paper on capital investment.

Apart from the 'commuter' lines of the Southern from London to Brighton and Portsmouth, no trunk line electrification had as yet been undertaken in Great Britain, except the LNER 1,500 V scheme between Sheffield and Manchester. Had Sir Vincent Raven of the North Eastern Railway lived and become Chief Mechanical Engineer of the LNER instead of Sir Nigel Gresley, the whole of the main line between Kings Cross and Edinburgh might have been electrified before the War. The NER had intended to electrify the stretch between York and Newcastle and Raven had built a magnificent prototype 2–Co–2 electric locomotive in 1922 which was far in advance of its time.

Sir Eustace Missenden, Chairman of the Railway Executive, expressed the opinion, in a paper to the Institute of Transport of November 1949, that the best prospect for railway motive power lay with electrification. In 1950 a committee, of which C. M. Cock (Riddles' Chief Officer, Electrical Engineering) was chairman, brought out a report on railway electrification which showed that 43·4 per cent of British Railways' route mileage had a traffic density in excess of what was computed to justify electrification on economic grounds. Later in the year Cock was succeeded by S. B. Warder, also late of the Southern Railway, who read a paper on Electric Traction Prospects before the Institution of Locomotive Engineers in December 1950. Introducing his paper, Warder pointed out that the unbalanced state of the national economy precluded any immediate possibility of developing electric traction in a big way; whilst technically and economically, he said, electric traction prospects were good, politically they were bad.

In March 1951 Riddles was invited by the SNCF to attend a

Above: The *King George VI* on 'The Caledonian' express. *Below:* Twin diesel locomotives Nos. 1000 and 1001 climbing Shap

By kind permission of British Railways

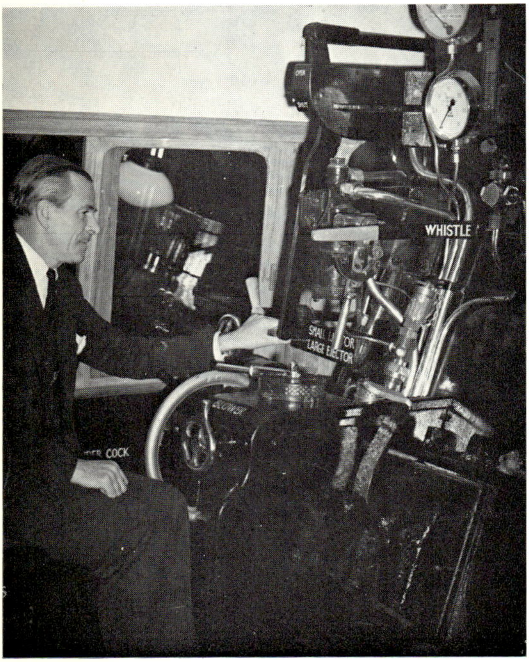

Above: Riddles, Cox and Bond

Left: Riddles in his 'mock-up' cab
By kind permission of British Railways

demonstration at Annecy on the 50 c/s trial route between Aix-le-Bains and La Roche-sur-Foron. He took with him his Chief Electrical Engineer, S. B. Warder. Also present were representatives of many British firms. Riddles was so impressed with the demonstration and with the whole concept of 50 c/s traction, that he invited the representatives of the British firms to a cocktail party and discussed with them the possibilities of introducing the system into Great Britain. It so happened that a few weeks earlier the Railway Executive had decided to abandon the electrified system on the line between Morecambe and Heysham and replace it by push-pull steam operation, as the equipment had worn out. Remembering this, Riddles said to his guests that if they would go back and persuade their principles to supply the equipment free, he would ask the Railway Executive to reverse their decision and would provide the vehicles and facilities to try out the system on the Heysham and Morecambe line. To this the firms' representatives agreed.

The nine-mile line between Heysham and Morecambe had been electrified in 1908 by the old Midland Railway to test the use of 25 c/s a.c. supply at 6,600 V. For rolling stock, Riddles provided three ex-LNWR three-coach electric train sets which had been built in 1914 and which had been made surplus by the closing to passenger traffic in 1940 of the Willesden-Earls Court line. These coaches were converted at Wolverton for their new role and each set comprised a motor coach, trailer, and driving trailer. The work of electrifying the line on the new system was carried out, under the direction of Warder, as a joint experiment in association with the British Electricity Authority, the English Electric Company, and British Insulated Callenders Cables. The investigation of interference, the cabling of overhead telephone and signal wires, and the modification of track circuits came under J. C. L. Train, the Railway Executive Member for Civil, Signal, and Telecommunications Engineering. The same voltage of 6,600 was retained temporarily for the 50 c/s electrification, but the new equipment was designed for 20 kV, as it was considered that this system would normally be used at the higher voltage. The first trains were being run in November 1952, within one year of starting the project, and full public electric service was started on August 17, 1953.

(It was subsequently Warder who was responsible for the electrification on the 50 c/s a.c. system of the whole of the old LNWR main line from Euston to Liverpool and Manchester, and he was awarded the Gold Medal of the Institution of Locomotive Engineers for his work on electrification—which was a very rare distinction.)

It would be appropriate now to examine the case for steam, as opposed to other forms of motive power, before discussing the so-called Standard steam locomotives that Riddles designed for British Railways. The responsibility for design, incidentally, is itself worth a moment's explanation. The relations between a CME and his Chief Draughtsman have been stated above. With a well organized and efficient drawing office and works, the amount of detailed design that a CME needs to undertake is comparatively little. It should suffice for him to lay down the broad lines of what he wants done, together with any necessary explanation of particular features. There have been statements in other books which appear to deny the credit for his engines to Riddles. Such statements are as unjustified as they would be if applied to the locomotives produced under, for instance, the regimes of Stanier and Churchward. One is reminded of the instruction which Churchward gave to Mr Holcroft (quoted in his book, *Locomotive Adventure*), 'Get me out a 2–6–0 with 5 feet 8 inches coupled wheels, outside cylinders and the No. 4 Boiler, and bring in all the standard parts you can'. And that is how the well-known Churchward 43XX class 2–6–0 was born. More generally, a CME stated his requirements in broad terms to the Chief Draughtsman, who translated these into more specific directions. The development draughtsmen then produced feasibility schemes, and finally the production drawing office converted them into working drawings. This was the kind of procedure used by and under Riddles, except that his requirements were dealt with by a body of Chief Draughtsmen instead of only one.

The case for steam received considerable attention in the pages of *The Railway Gazette* in 1969, and this discussion of the development of the steam locomotive some twenty years after Riddles started planning his own engines is of interest in showing how far his faith in the future of the steam engine was justified.

In March 1969 Ing L. D. Porta presented to the Institution of

Locomotive Engineers a paper entitled *Steam Locomotive Development in Argentina*, in which he described the encouraging results obtained by modifications to a number of steam locomotives on gauges from 2 feet 6 inches to 5 feet 6 inches. The work had been undertaken to the recommendations of M André Chapelon, Ing J. Vittone, and Ing L. D. Porta, and it included modifying the draughting, improving the steam circuit, and, in the later engines, introducing the gas producer technique to combustion.

Porta described a prototype metre-gauge compound 4–8–0 that had been rebuilt to his designs from a 4–6–2 and which, as a result, had developed an exceptionally high output. In all, locomotives of nine different classes of different gauges had been modified, including three 2–10–2s of the Rio Turbio mineral railway in Patagonia. These latter engines regularly hauled trains of 1,700 tons over a line on which the axleload was restricted to 7½ tons; and on trials 3,100 tons had been hauled on level track.

The metre gauge 4–8–0 hauled loads of up to 2,000 tons at 50 mph and 1,200 tons at 65 mph. (The condition of the track did not allow of the engine running at its designed speed of 75 mph.) The fuel consumption was extremely low. A class of thirty oil-fired 5 feet 6 inches gauge 2–6–2 tank engines on the Roca Railway were also rebuilt in a similar fashion, with the result that their maximum output was nearly doubled and their performance became comparable to that of the PS11 class three-cylinder Pacifics, which had a normal boiler capacity twice that of the tank engines. On express services the tank engines worked trains hitherto hauled by the 12E class Pacifics and burnt 23–25 lbs. of oil per mile as compared with 43–50 lbs. of the latter. The modifications introduced in the rebuilding included the provision of a Kylpor exhaust which increased the evaporation rate and cut the back pressure.

Another remarkable rebuilding was that of a three-cylinder 4–8–0 engine of class 11C, which had been supplied to the 5 feet 6 inches Roca Railway in the late 1920s. This was modified under the direction of M. Chapelon at the extraordinarily low cost of only 15 per cent of a general overhaul. It was so successful that the whole class of 75 engines were similarly modified. The increase in output at the drawbar was from 26 to 40 per cent. The improvements were due to 50 per cent better steam distribution, 30 per cent better draughting, and 16 per cent improved combustion. The rebuilt engines could handle 2,000 tons as compared with 1,500 before modification and with a reduction of 30 per cent in fuel consumption. They eventually replaced the later 15A and 15B class 4–8–0s, which were far more modern and more powerful than the 11C in its original form, in the haulage of the 1,000-ton fast fruit trains between the Rio Negro Valley and Buenos Aires, a distance of 740 miles.

The 2–10–2 locomotives, mentioned above, belonged to a batch built for the 2 feet 5½ inches gauge Rio Turbio Railway in 1956. This is a lightly built mineral line of 160 miles in Patagonia, and laid with rails of only 35 lbs. per yard. A second batch of these engines was built by the Japanese firm of Mitsubishi in 1964 incorporating the modifications made to the three in the first batch. These included a new firebox which incorporated Porta's gas producer combustion system in which most of the air is admitted above the fuel bed. With this arrangement secondary air is introduced through the sides of the firebox as well as the firehole and amounted to about 70 per cent of the total. Beneath the bars a small proportion of the exhaust steam is fed in to mix with the primary air and reduce the temperature of the fire bed. The fire bed is always dull red, showing that most of the heat is liberated in the combustion space. The sustained output was increased from 700 drawbar horse power to 1,200.

André Chapelon wrote a letter commenting on this paper in the September 5th issue of *The Railway Gazette*, and through his kindness and the courtesy of the Editor I am permitted to reproduce it.

After his opening remarks, M Chapelon continues:

'Mr Porta is eminent amongst those who believe in the further development of the steam locomotive. He has worked with perseverance towards this end, having incorporated in this prototype locomotive [i.e. the metre gauge 4–8–0] the majority of developments applied by the former Paris-Orléans railway from 1929, especially a steam circuit of large cross-section, high superheat and efficient draughting using the Kylchap exhaust, together with re-superheat between h.p. and l.p. cylinders previously applied successfully by the SNCF in 1940 to its 2–12–0 locomotive.

'The excellent results given by Mr Porta's metre gauge 4–8–0 have confirmed again the great importance of these design features which, re-superheat excepted, had enabled the continuous power output at the tender drawbar of the Paris-Orléans Pacifics to be increased from 1,450 to 2,700 hp at 68 mph. This was an increase of 86 per cent whilst specific fuel consumption was reduced from 5·28 to only 2·42 lb/dbhp/h at 1450 dbhp.

'The subsequent work of Mr Porta shows what can be achieved with well designed steam locomotives, even with a track gauge as narrow as the 2 feet 5½ inches gauge Rio Turbio Railway, where a 2–10–2 locomotive with 24 square feet grate area and an engine weight of 48 tons has been developed to haul a 3,000 ton track with outputs of 1,200 dbhp despite the use of poor quality fuel.

'One may ask whether the advance of later forms of traction which their advocates believed to be inevitable may not now be halted, especially in countries with limited financial resources where indigenous fuel often of poor quality can be used economically for steam traction.

'For example, developments in the USA could have been otherwise had it been possible to wait, and had more importance been attached to the tests carried out by the New York Central in 1946. The tests compared the results given by diesel and modern steam locomotives operating from modern depot installations on identical services and were described in Mr P. W. Kiefer's book *A practical evaluation of Railroad Motive Power* published in New York in 1947.

'Availability and monthly mileages for the steam locomotive tested reached 90 per cent of those for diesels. Thus, one is far from the often cited ratios of three or even four steam locomotives being replaced by one diesel, because modern diesels have been compared with obsolescent steam locomotives confusing the effects of modernization with changes in traction.

'The most significant results of the New York Central tests were in the comparisons of total operating costs which showed that, for equivalent service, the total annual cost per mile was $1·22 for a steam 4–8–4 of 6,000 nominal hp, $1.11 for a twin-unit diesel of 4,000 hp, $1.48 for a triple-unit diesel of 6,000 hp, and $1.15 for an electric locomotive of 5,000 hp continuous rating with the important qualification that the last figure did not include the appreciable maintenance costs for sub-stations and the overhead contact system.

'The steam locomotives used, the Niagara type with 102 square feet grate area, were built from 1945 onwards and were capable of sustaining 5,050 dbhp continuously at 62 mph. The three-cylinder compound SNCF 4–8–4 locomotive with a grate area of 54 square feet only but having high superheat, a steam circuit of large cross-section and triple Kylchap exhaust, developed 4,000 dbhp continuously at the same speed. This worked out at 74 dbhp per square foot grate compared with 49 dbhp per square foot for the Niagara, an increase of 50 per cent.

'Had the Niagara locomotive incorporated the basic design features applied to the SNCF locomotive it should have been able to sustain continuously 7,500 dbhp, which would have necessitated five 2,000 hp diesel units to provide equivalent performance. The ratios of equivalence between diesel and steam units mentioned would then have been transformed and the investment charges of an equivalent diesel fleet would be very much greater.

'Even with the 4,000 hp diesel units which are being developed it would still be necessary to provide three such units to obtain equivalent power. It is interesting to recall that a 4,000 hp diesel unit develops about 2,500 dbhp at 75 mph, whilst the "Pacifics" of the former Paris-Orléans, built 60 years ago, developed this power at the tender drawbar after their rebuilding twenty years later.

'The development of the steam locomotive was still far from its limits when the last American Mallets were built and developed over 7,000 dbhp. Within the same overall dimensions and using the improved design features mentioned their power could have been increased to at least 11,000 dbhp. By adopting triple-expansion in conjunction with boiler pressure of 570 lbs per square inch and a water-tube firebox of the type developed successfully by Lawford Fry together with re-superheat this could be increased to reach 15,000 dbhp.

'The stock argument against the steam locomotive has been on the thermal efficiency at the drawbar, often citing 6 per cent for steam, 22 per cent for diesel, and 17 per cent for electric traction. These differences are often nullified when one takes account of the cost of energy at the locomotive, which often varies in inverse ratio to thermal efficiency with the resultant cost per hp/h remaining very much the same for all three traction systems.

'With electric traction one should not underestimate the incidence of transmission and distribution losses between power station and the locomotive pantograph. Combined with energy loss in generation, total losses may easily total 80 per cent for an average size supply network.

'Thus, one may arrive at the paradox that it is preferable to transport coal from the mine by train hauled by steam locomotives rather than to generate electrical energy at the pit-head and supply it through transmission lines. A train with a payload of 1,500 tons of 2,000 tons gross would involve a consumption of 10 tons to cover 125 miles, whilst for the transmission of a corresponding quantity of energy by high-tension lines with a transmission loss of about 15 per cent, the equivalent energy loss would be 225 tons, 22·5 times greater than that of the coal consumed.

'Neither is the problem of diesel traction maintenance costs negligible, because lengthy experience, as on the Pennsylvania for example, shows that costs increase twice as rapidly as those for steam traction and reduce considerably the length of economic life with diesels.

'The capacity of diesel locomotives for rapid acceleration at low speed is of great value for shunting and transfer work but is of little relevance at normal running speeds in main line service at which equivalent steam locomotives develop their maximum power. For example, a J.3 class 4–6–4 of the New York Central rated at 4,700 ihp took 2·28 minutes to accelerate to 35 mph in 0·7 mile which compares with 1·42 minutes and 0·5 mile for a 4,000 hp twin-unit diesel. To attain 80 mph the J.3 required 9·76 minutes covering 8·6 miles, against 14·17 min. and 14·8 miles for the diesel unit. The trailing load was 900 tons in each case.

'In France the most recent Mikado locomotives gave continuous outputs at the drawbar of 2,000 hp at 60 mph and the output could be raised to 3,000 hp if need be. Outputs beyond the predetermined figure cannot be obtained with diesels, nor is it possible to take advantage of short-term peak outputs which steam engines can provide.

'Diesel and electric locomotives with freely rotating bogies, an excessively low centre of gravity, and a too low rolling frequency for the locomotive as a whole, inflict on the track lateral forces which increase with speed. These undesirable reactions, which increase the wear on the track, both reduce passenger comfort and increase maintenance costs. They may even produce deformations resulting ultimately in derailments.

'If one has become accustomed, with electric traction, to a number of failures per kilometre run which, including those attributable to the distribution and catenary systems, is double that for a steam locomotive fleet of much greater average age, diesel traction has substantially surpassed these figures. It is understood that in some countries the number of diesel locomotives out of service at depots, either for lack of spare parts or awaiting heavy overhaul, has been up to 40 per cent of the total stock.

'Whilst there is still time, action should be taken to modernize the greatest possible number of steam locomotives with the advantages which Mr Porta has illustrated yet again. This will avoid further very heavy investment charges and, at the same time, allow design departments to prepare new projects taking advantage of all the latest developments in technology.'

In the face of this powerful argument by one of the greatest locomotive engineers of any age, there can surely be few who would now criticize Riddles for choosing steam traction under the conditions and at the time when he had to make a decision. It may be that a large number will even consider it to have been little less than absurd to destroy a fleet of modern steam engines, after only a short life, in the name of modernization. In Great Britain, electrification would have had to replace steam in due course, because the limits imposed by the British loading gauge would not have permitted locomotives of dimensions large enough to provide the power necessary for greatly increased speeds.

CHAPTER XV

'C M E' Policy

In approaching the difficult job which confronted him, Riddles had been heartened by a letter from his great old chief, Admiral Sir Harold Brown. He wrote: 'I am sorry I missed the opportunity the other day to congratulate you on your recent appointment; anyhow I do now. Just about the biggest engineering job going at present and I can imagine no one more fitted to fill it.'

Before deciding a programme for the construction of locomotives, carriages, and wagons, Riddles had to determine the method of tackling the task. He could have elected to do nothing constructive himself and to leave the initiative for design split between the former main line companies, so that development and construction followed the separate pre-nationalization policies without any common standardization. There were some very vocal advocates of that solution; but the result would have been that for each traffic purpose four different kinds of locomotive or carriage would have been produced. And these would have been different in every component, made of materials having different specifications for the same purpose, and generally unable to run freely outside the region of their origin due to weight and loading gauge limitations. The adoption of such an uneconomical procedure would have been severely criticized. Excluding this solution, there were three possible choices: to select the designs of one of the former companies as the standard for British Railways, to nominate for each traffic category the best of an existing type for all future construction, or to develop a completely new range of standard designs. The first of the above was ruled out, because the products of each of the former companies had reached a high standard of development and no one company was indisputably pre-eminent. The choice between the other two required careful consideration.

As regards locomotives; a policy committee was set up by Riddles on January 8, 1948, to make recommendations, covering firstly the standardization of fittings and equipment and secondly the possibility of selecting in each traffic category the best existing regional type for all future construction in that category. In conjunction with this investigation, Riddles arranged with Barrington-Ward to have trials of different types of locomotive in three traffic categories on trains and under conditions which were as nearly identical as possible, running on various lines of the different regions. He stressed that all reports should be prepared in the same way and supported by dynamometer records, and that all the results should be made available, not only to the regions, but also to the general public—for there was considerable partisan feeling, as between the former companies and their locomotives, by the large body of railway enthusiasts (or 'railwayacs', as Riddles terms the fraternity).

The interchange trials which followed took place between April and September 1948. The three traffic categories and the fourteen locomotives which took part were as follows:

a. Express Passenger: LMS, Stanier Duchess class Pacific and rebuilt Royal Scot class 4–6–0; LNE, Gresley A4 class streamlined Pacific; GW, Collett King class 4–6–0; and S, Bulleid Merchant Navy class Pacific.

b. Mixed Traffic: LMS, Stanier class 5 4–6–0; LNE, Thompson B1 class 4–6–0; GW, Collett Hall class 4–6–0; and S, Bulleid West Country class Pacific.

c. Heavy Freight: LMS, Stanier class 8F 2–8–0; LNE, Gresley O2 class three-cylinder 2–8–0; GW, Churchward 28XX class 2–8–0; WD, Riddles 2–10–0; and WD, Riddles 2–8–0.

The Great Western engines, owing to the width over their cylinders, could only run over GW and LNE routes.

Riddles' insistence on a wide publicity was well justified because the trials showed that no one regional type was so superior to the others as to be an obvious selection for standard production. There were indeed marginal differences, but many of them were caused by either methods of driving or by the weather. In general all did the work for which they were designed. An interesting sidelight was that it was shown, as Riddles had long suspected, that there were no geographical limitations to the use of any one type. The Southern West Country Pacific, for instance, was just as much at home in the Highlands of Scotland as the locomotives that had been specially designed for these mountainous routes. It proved, incidentally, the correctness of Stanier's policy of building standard engines for use all over the LMS system, as compared with Gresley's practice of designing engines 'tailor made' for different geographical areas.

In design the Locomotive Standards Committee found that the margin between different regions was as close as that displayed in the inter-change trials, and they were unable to recommend the adoption of any one type. However, some classes were clearly excluded on account of either loading gauge or weight restrictions. Thus, as we have seen, Great Western engines could not run over the erstwhile LMS lines and LNER engines generally carried heavier axle loads than locomotives of other Regions in the same traffic category. An additional factor was that, though a wide range of fittings could be standardized on new locomotives, they would entail considerable alterations if used on existing engines. A further difficulty was the strong regional objection to any locomotive or fitting imported from another region. This was not confined to CMEs and their immediate assistants, for the men themselves objected strongly to 'foreign' engines.

As a result of all these factors Riddles came to the conclusion that he would have to develop a series of new engines. The only policy question remaining, therefore, was what type of engines. In a lecture delivered before the Graduates' Section of the Institution of Mechanical Engineers on January 24, 1953, Riddles outlined the choice that was continuously facing those who had the responsibility of making decisions; the choice between developing existing and well-tried designs or of launching into something entirely new. It entailed the ability to assess those developments which would be of lasting value, and those which, though new, were not necessarily superior to existing and well-tried practices. It demanded the moral courage to be indifferent to criticism for either excessive conservatism or unwarranted rashness. It needed dispassionate judgment to weigh the merits of a new and exciting idea against the safer evolution from records, comparisons, trials, and assessments of costs. The former might yield results that would change the whole future of locomotive design, but it might also lead to 'the last dismal scene in the scrap yard where the acetylene flame cuts through the smart body on which so much money and hope has been lost'. The latter would lead to progress, but it would be slow and conservative. Sound progress has always been a mixture of the two, and it is the successful engineer who can decide the correct proportions. 'If one takes the broadest view of rail traction, the really outstandingly successful innovations of widest application in the past 100 years can be counted almost on the fingers of one hand, while the failures have been countless.'

These were the considerations which guided Riddles in the design of his engines. The post-war circumstances demanded engines which, though incorporating all that was best in modern practice, should be simple to drive, easy to maintain, and able to run with indifferent fuel: embodying, in fact, some of the reasoning which lay behind George Whale's Precursors.

Riddles decided that in the higher power range his engines would be of entirely new design. In the lower power range, however, it happened that the LMS alone amongst the former companies, had towards the end of its existence produced the three classes of small engines already mentioned. They contained every modern feature, had proved remarkably successful, and were built to dimensions and axle-weights which enabled them to run over most routes throughout the country. There could not be the same objection to using them on other regions because they had no modern competitors. It was decided, therefore, to include them, with only detail modifications, in the standard range. (But there was an amusing sequel. Mr J. N. Maskelyne, in his book *Locomotives I have Known* with a foreword by Riddles, records that a new LMS class 2 MT 2–6–0 engine was sent to the Western Region in 1949 to be tried in comparison with the GWR 2301 class goods engines, mentioned in Chapter IX. The drivers reported that the 2–6–0 was the inferior of the two, and this was confirmed by tests carried out at Swindon! The matter was reported in a paper on *Locomotive Testing on British Railways*, read before the Institution of Locomotive Engineers on September 20, 1950, by Mr D. A. Carling and during Riddles' Presidential Year. The 2–6–0 had been designed to burn hard coal and would not steam with Welsh coal, for which the maximum draught was too low. As a result of studies carried out in the Swindon drawing office, the trouble was cured by fitting a specially made liner inside the existing chimney. In fairness it must be added that this class of engine had performed excellently and steamed freely on the London Midland, Eastern and North Eastern regions. Nevertheless, this incident illustrates the problems that had to be surmounted in building inter-regional engines.)

Studies led to the conclusion that twelve different locomotive types would meet all the requirements of British Railways, replacing some hundreds of classes. Standard fittings would be used for all engines, and, in accordance with Riddles' maxim of 'get-at-ability', only two cylinders would be used where they would suffice for the job, and these and their valve gear would be outside. Wide fireboxes would be incorporated, where practicable, to obtain good steaming with poor coal, to raise the maximum steam production, and to lower the rate of combustion.

The immediate locomotive need was for a passenger engine of some 30,000 to 35,000 lbs. tractive effort. The top passenger range was covered adequately by Pacifics of three of the old companies and by the 4–6–0 *Kings* of the GWR. A longer term need was for a heavy freight locomotive. The remaining nine types could have been met by existing regional classes, but for the objections already stated. The broad plan was therefore as follows:

The first six types, to be constructed in 1951, were:

Class 7	4–6–2 Mixed Traffic with 20¼-ton axle-load.
Class 6	4–6–2 Mixed Traffic with 18½-ton axle-load.
Class 5	4–6–0 Mixed Traffic with 19-ton axle-load.
Class 4	4–6–0 Mixed Traffic with 17-ton axle-load.
Class 4	2–6–4T Mixed Traffic with 18-ton axle-load.
Class 3	2–6–2T Mixed Traffic with 16¼-ton axle-load.

Four more types were to be introduced when required, and of these the first three listed were to be existing LMS classes with only detail modifications:

Class 4	2–6–0 Mixed Traffic with 16¾-ton axle-load.
Class 2	2–6–0 Mixed Traffic with 13-ton axle-load.
Class 2	2–6–2T Mixed Traffic with 13-ton axle-load.
Class 3	2–6–0 Mixed Traffic with 16-ton axle-load.

Finally, there were two more types which would not be required for some time because there were already sufficient regional locomotives in existence to meet traffic needs. These were:

A Heavy Express Passenger Locomotive with 22½-ton axle-load.
A Heavy Freight Locomotive with 17-ton axle-load.

In this range great emphasis was placed on the capacity for mixed traffic working and in providing modern engines for light as well as for heavy duties.

As a result of the decision to build these standard locomotives new sets of drawings had to be made and a good many new tools were necessary. Policy committees were set up to establish the new components. In forming all these committees Riddles was following the practice of his earlier days, when he had collected together men to advise the foreman and made them inspectors. In principle, he hated committees, but under the circumstances there was no alternative; and the results justified them, for the outcome of their work was the adoption of the cream of all locomotive practices in the country. The committee of Chief Draughtsmen which he had assembled under Cox got all the answers he wanted in a comparatively short time. Answers to his questions as to efficiency in operation, manufacture, maintenance, and costs were agreed and given by men who would be responsible for working out the detail design. Workshop committees were also set up for various activities, and the results obtained in the white metal, bronze, and brass section alone saved an estimated £1,000,000 a year.

The establishment by Riddles of an entirely separate carriage and wagon section under Pugson had been objected to by some, but the decision was soon shown to be justified. The carriage and wagon engineers were delighted at playing a role which was no longer minor to the locomotive interests, and their enthusiasm and consequent cooperation was a major factor in success.

Some work on the possible standardization of the principal dimensions had already been undertaken by the CMEs of the former companies, in conjunction with the respective civil engineers, and a 63 feet 6 inches coach length had been tentatively proposed. Because of the serious loading gauge restrictions on certain regions, the width of 9 feet at the waist had to be reduced to 8 feet $2\frac{7}{8}$ inches at cornice height, which gave an undesirable 'tumble-home' to the body sides. After nationalization these proposals were re-examined and the civil engineers were eventually able to submit a loading gauge allowing almost universal running, with a width at cornice height of 8 feet 8 inches, which was very close to the existing regional cross-sections.

It was decided in these new coaches to offer the travelling public the highest level of constructional safety economically obtainable; and to this end three features were laid down: firstly, an all-steel construction, in which underframe, body framing, and roof and panels were of steel, with wide use of welding; secondly, the use of Buckeye couplers and Pullman gangways, which had shown their ability to hold a train together more satisfactorily in an accident; and thirdly, doubling the resistance of the vehicle to end loading, without any increase in weight if possible. The development of the steel carriage with prefabricated sides and integral structure was a real 'break-through'. The standard carriage was increased in strength and reduced in weight, in spite of carrying half a ton more water.

The policy that had been applied to locomotives was also followed for carriages; carrying out intensive investigations and dividing this work and the resulting design between the regions. Riding tests were instituted on the former Great Central main line with bogies designed by each of the former companies and with both new and worn tyres. These led to the production of prototype bogies made up of the best of Great Western and London & North Eastern practice, and these were also tested as new, part worn and worn. The results were then handed over to the research department for investigation into possible improvement. A full-size prototype underframe was subjected to end loads up to 200 tons, with strain gauge measurements taken at fifty places, and similar tests were carried out on two regional type frames for comparison.

For design and production, four separate committees were set up, each composed of appropriate members from all regions. These were for, respectively: carriage production, dealing with tools, equipments, and methods; carriage standards, with the task of reviewing existing practice and recommending standards for new coaches in general and in detail; power brake, to deal with all aspects affecting brakes; and train lighting, including all electrical equipment on coaching vehicles. There was also an *ad hoc* committee on interior decoration, which included officers of the operating and commercial departments and the railway executive architect.

The ultimate cost of maintenance was borne in mind at every stage of construction, and indeed costs figured largely in every aspect of operating carriages. Pugson, as an old LMS man, was very conscious of costs. One day, for instance, he came to Riddles and pointed out that if the one yellow line which was painted round the body of the non-passenger vehicle stock could be abolished, there would be an annual saving of £2,000. 'Cut it out, Puggy', said Riddles; and nobody apparently noticed the difference.

The Transport Commission had a very good and high level Scientific Commission, the members of which were drawn from a wide field and included Stanier. Riddles was being pressed to build coaches which were even lighter than those he had produced. He explained that it was necessary to have strength in buffing and great resistance to telescoping. But this argument was not fully accepted, and opinions were expressed that the aircraft industry, with their knowledge of light alloys, would be able to help. To this Riddles retorted that, apart from the cost, no aeroplane had yet pulled seventeen others behind it, nor had had to stop these seventeen other aeroplanes. However, the exponents of aircraft techniques persisted. Stanier said to him, 'Robert, it's better to please a fool than to tease him; let them have a go'. Riddles accordingly got into touch with a big aircraft firm and gave them a drawing of a standard coach. He stipulated that the coach must have a buffing stress of 200 tons and resistance to telescoping. Three months later he asked the firm how they were getting on; to which they replied that they had so many of their own design commitments that they were unable to put forward a scheme. Stanier was right!

In the 1951 building programme almost all the corridor stock was built to the new British Railway standards, and there were the following twelve different body styles: third class corridor, third class corridor brake, first class corridor, composite corridor, composite corridor brake, third class open with fixed seating, third

Above: Unveiling of the *Britannia* at Marylebone Station. *Left* to *right*: Sir Eustace Missenden, Lord Hurcomb, R. A. Riddles, Rt. Hon. Alfred Barnes (Minister of Transport)

Below: Britannia and *Cornwall*, Riddles has endorsed this photograph; 'I have driven both of them'

By kind permission of British Railways

Above: Britannia Class Pacific the *William Shakespeare* on the 'Golden Arrow' Pullman Car express. *Below:* Britannia Class Pacific No. 70045 on the 'Emerald Isle Express'

By kind permission of British Railways

class open with loose seating, first class open with fixed seating, first class open with loose seating, kitchen car, restaurant car with kitchen and loose seating, passenger brake van.

In the very early days of nationalization Sir Cyril Hurcomb asked Riddles what colour they should paint the engines. Riddles replied that the only proper colour for a locomotive was black. Hurcomb thought this rather dull, but Riddles pointed out that it was the most economical colour because engines so painted would not need to be painted again for another ten years; in addition a damaged panel could be replaced without having to repaint the whole engine, which was necessary if the engine was of any other colour because of the difficulty of matching. Further, the old London & North Western engines, with their lining out, had looked very smart indeed. Hurcomb was not convinced and much controversy arose, with various people airing their own ideas on the subject. At that time an additional argument in favour of black was that owing to the shortage of cleaners the engines were generally dirty, and there seemed little point in spending more money on a colour which would soon be obscured with grime. However, with Stanier's advice in mind about taking the easy road, Riddles told his critics that they could choose what colours they liked and he would have some engines painted for them to make a final selection. Black was not one of the choices! On January 30, 1948, there were duly lined up at Addison Road Station, Kensington, four Stanier Class 5 4–6–0s, painted variously in the green liveries of the LNER, Great Western, and Southern, and in Caledonian blue. There was considerable discussion but no consensus of opinion. When the distinguished gathering was about to depart, Riddles announced that he had one more engine to show. 'Then', he says, 'I called up from round the corner, literally from round the corner, another Class 5. She was beautifully painted in a glistening 'blackberry' black, lined out in the old LNWR red, grey and yellow, and with all the steel work polished. There was a moment's silence; and then a very eminent person ejaculated, "Riddles, you b——!".' I saw this engine myself a short time afterwards at Crewe and she looked absolutely magnificent. The result of the 'parade' was that 19,000 engines were painted black and some 2,000 in other colours.

The public was given an opportunity to choose the colours for the carriages. Hussey showed me the various liveries from which the choice was to be made, during a visit that I paid to Riddles' offices. We both, and Riddles, hoped that the 'plum and spilt milk' of the London & North Western would be selected. The trial train in these colours was certainly by far the most attractive, but the public was not interested. None of the liveries demonstrated was eventually chosen; instead it was decided to paint the carriages red and cream—a choice so horrible that after a comparatively short time it was decently covered by LMS maroon.

CHAPTER XVI

The Riddles Engines

In the previous chapter are listed the types of locomotives which it was decided should be constructed for British Railways. Amongst the principles that Riddles stated for the design of these engines were that they should have the greatest steam-producing capacity that weight and dimensions permitted; that all working parts should be simple, visible and get-at-able; and that each class should be able to work mixed traffic over the widest possible range. It was decided that all should have two cylinders (except the heavy express passenger engine, which would need more to produce the power required), primarily because two outside cylinders provide the most visible and accessible arrangement.

In 1949 there were established two constructional gauges which were designated L_1 and L_2. Of these the former was designed to fit the loading gauge of any line in Great Britain, whilst the latter was larger and permitted movement over nearly all the main lines. It was decided that all locomotives of Class 4 and below should be able to run on any line that their axle weight allowed, whilst Class 5 and upwards need only conform to the larger construction gauge.

The establishment of these two gauges was a great achievement by the Civil Engineers, and showed how well the two departments were working together. Riddles' rolling stock plans depended absolutely on the production of such a scheme, and the speed with which it was completed was invaluable.

A minor but essential psychological point was that there should be a family resemblance between all the engines and that they should resemble those of any one region as little as possible—though there was inevitably a closer visual affinity to the later engines of the LMS than to any others. It was obviously desirable that a complete design should be allotted to one drawing office, but this in itself could lead to almost unintentional perpetuation of previous company practice. To get over this, and since he wanted components standardized as far as possible, Riddles decided to give each drawing office a dual role: to be parent to one or more locomotive types and to design components for all types.

The allocation of the first six classes of locomotives for construction in 1951 and some of the components to the four drawing offices was as follows:

Brighton—Class 4 4–6–0, Class 4 2–6–4T, brake and sanding gear.
Swindon—Class 3 2–6–2T, steam fittings, boiler and smokebox mountings, etc.
Doncaster—Class 5 4–6–0, coupling and connecting rods, cylinders and valve gear.
Derby—Class 6 and 7 4–6–2, bogies and trucks, wheels, axles and axleboxes.

The two Pacifics were entirely new designs. The chassis was the same for both, except that the Class 6 had smaller cylinders; the boiler of the Class 6 had a maximum diameter of 6 feet 1 inch with a pressure of 225 lbs., as compared with the 6 feet 5½ inches and pressure of 250 lbs. for the Class 7; and the grate areas for the Classes 6 and 7 were 36 square feet and 42 square feet respectively. The Class 7 engine was intended to do the same work as the Great Western *Castle*, the LMS rebuilt *Royal Scot*, the LNER *Green Arrow* 2–6–2, and the Southern *West Country* Pacific. The Class 6 Pacific was intended for routes on which a powerful locomotive was required, but where axle load restrictions prohibited the use of the Class 7. The Class 5 4–6–0 was a general mixed traffic engine, having the boiler of the LMS Class 5, though modified slightly, and intended for similar duties. This class had a slightly heavier axle weight than the Class 6. The Class 4 2–6–4 tank engine was developed from the very similar LMS engine; but to enable it to pass the L_1 construction gauge, the cylinders were reduced in size and, to obtain the same power, the boiler pressure was increased. The LMS boiler was retained, though stayed for the higher pressure, but most of the rest of the engine entailed new design. The Class 4 4–6–0 was a tender version of the 2–6–4T for longer distance runs on L_1 gauge railways, and fitted with a leading bogie. (Because there was no bogie at the trailing end, it was considered that one was needed in front as giving better guiding than a pony truck.) The Class 3 2–6–2–tank engine was designed to fill a need for an engine mid-way in power and axle load between the Class 4 and the LMS Class 2 designs (which were to become standard). It had the Swindon No. 4 boiler, but modified with greater superheat and a dome.

All these locomotives had rocking grates, self-cleaning smokeboxes, and self-emptying ashpans. Copper fireboxes were used, because, owing to the variation in the quality of water available, they gave better service than steel. The well-tried and reliable Walschaerts valve gear was chosen and fitted outside.

Draughting had been the subject of tests at Rugby and Swindon, and that adopted was based on the finding of these tests. It had been shown that double, and other special, blast pipe arrangements could give improved results at maximum output, but were inferior in their performance at lower outputs, and through the whole range were less satisfactory than the single blast pipe. Because, therefore, the majority of locomotive work demands less than the maximum output, the single blast pipe and chimney were retained on most of the engines. Work carried out by S. O. Ell at Swindon demonstrated that quite minor modifications to the size and shape of the single chimney could effect a vast increase in performance. (The ideal Ell chimney was very slender, so that for the sake of appearance the locomotives had chimneys with double-walled castings, the outside wall being of large diameter.) Ell was, says Riddles, an exceptional engineer, and his work and research did much to improve the performance of locomotives. He was in charge of the Swindon testing plant where he achieved the most invaluable results.

To arrive at the right cab design Riddles had a full-scale mock-up of the back of the engine and front of the tender built at Derby, in order that those who would have to drive the engines should have a chance to express their opinions on the proposed layout. The mock-up was brought to Marylebone and installed in the headquarters of the Railway Executive on December 5, 1949. There it was inspected, discussed, and criticized by motive power superintendents, running shed foremen, drivers, and union representatives. It was Riddles intention that the driver should be able to operate the locomotive entirely from a sitting position; and the regulator, brake, and all the other controls managed by the driver were so placed that he could do this. The reversing wheel was normally sited broadside on to the driver, but Riddles with, as he says, his 'domestic' mind, had the reversing wheel placed end on, on the grounds that no woman could manage a mangle wheel in the broadside position. In general the cab arrangements were accepted. The feature which surprised and pleased some of the Great Western drivers was that it would be possible to drive sitting down, which they had never been able to do on their own engines.

The next four types of engine to be built were the Class 4 2–6–0 allocated to Doncaster), the Class 2 2–6–0 (to Derby), the Class 2 2–6–2T (to Derby), and the Class 3 2–6–0 (to Swindon). As has been said, the first three were LMS engines with minor modifications. The Class 3 2–6–0 was a tender version of the Class 3 2–6–2T, and it was given the same modified Swindon boiler as the latter.

In October 1952 there was the bad smash at Harrow in which the LMS Pacific No. 46202 was completely wrecked. This engine had only recently been rebuilt from Stanier's *Turbomotive*, and its destruction left a gap in the number of Class 8 Pacifics in the London Midland Region. This gave Riddles the opportunity to ask and obtain authority to build a new Class 8 Pacific with which running experience might be gained for a future building of standard Class 8 engines. And so came No. 71000 *Duke of Gloucester*, the only one of the class ever built. The engine had three cylinders with Caprotti valve gear and the same boiler as the Class 7 Pacifics, but with a bigger grate.

The last of the twelve types was the heavy freight engine. The Chief Draughtsmen's Committee had proposed a 2–8–2. This Riddles disliked, because with such a wheel arrangement adhesion would be lost and there would be little gained in this respect over the existing 2–8–0s. In the light of the experience of his previous very successful ten-coupled freight engine, he said that he wanted a 2–10–0, but that he would like confirmation that 5 feet coupled wheels could be used with a wide firebox. Investigation showed this to be possible and the 2–10–0 was therefore built. The coupled wheel base was given the same form of flexibility as that of the Austerity engine. This was the most revolutionary of all Riddles' locomotives, because experience from the others had been made use of in its design. (Riddles gave instructions that this engine was to have the same chimney as he had put on his Austerity engines, but by the time the 2–10–0 appeared he had retired and the instruction was not carried out. The reason is something of a mystery. F. G. Carrier made an arrangement drawing of the locomotive, which is no longer in existence, but the diagram by K. W. Everett which accompanied it shows the Austerity chimney.) Riddles feels that his Class 6 Pacific was a mistake. Had he made it a 4–8–0, he believes that it would have provided a solution for passenger traffic problems in Scotland—problems with which he had become fully acquainted during his time at St Rollox.

Here, then, were the twelve classes of steam locomotives which were designed to meet all the traffic needs of British Railways. They incorporated, as Riddles had intended, all the best practice of the past. The inclusion of steam passages designed in accordance with Chapelon's principles, together with Ell's method of draughting, resulted in engines that were so free-running and efficient in steam production that no subsequent trials with such devices as Crosti boilers and Giesl ejectors resulted in anything more than marginal improvement. Furthermore, their simplicity and ease of maintenance, and the capacity of the bigger engines with their wide fireboxes to run with poor fuel, met the difficult conditions in Great Britain during the post-War years.

Riddles was not sanguine enough to expect these engines to be trouble-free. The design of a steam engine is more of an art than an exact science, and it only needed memories of the initial difficulties with Stanier's engines to deter too optimistic an outlook. Apart from this, the engines started at a disadvantage. The locomotive establishments of the old Companies could not be expected to welcome these strangers amongst their own competent locomotive studs, and the notoriously conservative drivers could be expected in many areas not only to resent the intrusion of such foreign engines, but, by not attempting to master them, make them appear failures. They could hardly, too, expect a welcome from the 'railwayacs', many of whom were fanatical followers of one or other of the old Companies and loathed nationalization and anything to do with it. There had been similar reactions at the time of the Grouping, when North Eastern drivers had complained that a Gresley Pacific would not steam, when Eastleigh men had resented the invasion of Ashford practices, and when Crewe had revolted over Midland red. Enthusiastic members and followers of the Great Western Railway, a company which had not been seriously affected by the Grouping, believed that the sun had stood still over locomotive development since the appearance of the Castle class over a quarter of a century before. The situation was not helped by the fact that many of the engines looked LMS, and indeed some were. The reasons for this have been explained.

In the circumstances of the time these twelve classes could be regarded as a first generation of British Railways steam locomotives. Riddles was looking ahead to a Great Britain in which all main lines would be electrified but this would of necessity be a lengthy process, and steam locomotives would be required, as on the Paris–Orléans, to run trains over the as yet non-electrified portions at electric schedules. (Had this policy been followed, he believes that by this time the West Coast, East Coast, and West of England main lines would have been electrified over the major part of their length. Branch line passenger services could be suitably operated by diesel multiple units, but there would remain a lengthy, if decreasing freight and express passenger mileage operated by steam.) There was still room for development of the steam locomotive inside the British loading gauge; better boiler proportions and draughting arrangements might have been provided, for instance Garratt locomotives might have been built to get more power. (Garratts had been unpopular on the LMS because Midland axleboxes and weak Midland frames had been insisted on by the then Midland dominated locomotive regime.) Even with existing power, steam-hauled expresses could have run much faster if the signalling had been improved, as it has been for diesel and electric operation.

Another factor which might tend to hasten electrification was the increasing difficulty in recruiting men to do the dirty job of cleaner, the bottom rung of the promotion ladder to driver and inspector. Both Stanier and Riddles foresaw problems in obtaining sufficient engine crews for steam locomotives. Nevertheless the

Above: Clan Class Pacific *Clan Campbell* near Tebay

Left: The first 50 c/s a.c. electric train to run in Britain, Riddles is in the driving compartment

By kind permission of British Railways

Above: 4–8–0 locomotive No. 240 P4. One of the last series of 25 engines rebuilt from the P.O. small-wheeled Pacifics. In a letter to the author M. Chapelon refers to them as the engines 'que j'ai particulièrement apprécié'

Below: M. André Chapelon with his 3-cylinder compound 4–8–4 No. 242 A1, as it came out of the works of the Forges et Acieries de la Marine et d'Homecourt in 1946

By kind permission of M. A. Chapelon

Above: A Riddles Class 5 showing Caprotti valve gear

Below: Class 9 2–10–0 No. 92000 in the Erecting Shop at Crewe

By kind permission of British Railways

Above: No. 92000 in the Erecting Shop at Crewe after being wheeled

Below: No 92000, the first of the Class 9 2–10–0 locomotives
By kind permission of British Railways

difficulty might have been overcome if sufficient prestige could have been attached to the job. (The way the author's unit tackled a recruiting difficulty is described in Chapter VI, but it is perhaps one which would not have been greeted with any enthusiasm by the Unions!)

The first of the Class 7 Pacifics, No. 70000, was steamed at Crewe on January 2, 1951, and on January 14th the engine ran to Carlisle on test with the dynamometer car and empty carriages. Cox was on the footplate for the northbound run, and Riddles and Bond were on it for the return journey to Crewe the following day, when Riddles drove the engine from Carlisle to Penrith, and Bond from Penrith to Crewe. The round trip was extremely successful. The engine was as yet unnamed, but on January 30th she was named *Britannia* at Marylebone by the Right Honourable Alfred Barnes, Minister of Transport. The name *Britannia* had been selected by Riddles and Hussey to commemorate the badge of Britannia and the Lion which was the emblem of the old London & North Western Railway; and Riddles had a small table made for the Minister as a memento of the occasion on which was an enamelled representation of this badge and the engine. (A duplicate of this table which was made in case of an accident is now in Riddles' home.) Hussey wanted to have a plaque of the emblem (presumably with the foliated surround which had earned Webb's Eighteen-inch Goods engines the name of 'Cauliflowers') placed on the engine; but Riddles decided that this might provoke some controversy, and the idea was not pursued.

There were 55 of the Britannias, of which 25 were completed in 1951, 20 more in 1952, and the final 10 in 1954. It had been intended, after much discussion, to fit roller bearings to all the coupled wheels. But Riddles was not convinced as to the superiority of roller bearings over the much cheaper LMS plain bearings. He therefore had five engines equipped with roller bearings on the driving axle only, and another ten with plain bearings throughout. It does not appear that the roller bearings showed any advantage over the plain type. Initial reception of the Britannias was, as expected, mixed. But that the new engines were, given a chance, outstanding, was shown by the results obtained in the area of the old Great Eastern Railway. Here their arrival enabled the whole express timetable to be reconstructed to show the fastest runs ever performed over Great Eastern tracks, and the third fastest average speeds over any section of British Railways. The drivers loved them and seemed to delight in making the most phenomenal runs. At the other end of the scale, the Great Western reception was distinctly chilly and results accordingly were patchy.

It is difficult, in fact, to think of many new express locomotives that have gone straight into service with so little trouble on the most exacting schedules. Gresley's Pacifics required considerable modification before they were really good, Stanier's first Pacifics needed much attention before they became the excellent machines that they soon were, and Bulleid's Pacifics had troubles that were never overcome until they were entirely rebuilt. The only major trouble experienced with the Britannias was with the driving wheels moving on the axles. This was comparatively easily cured by plugging the ends of the axles. A minor defect was a 'fore-and-aft' motion imparted to the train. This was found to be due to the drawbar spring at the rear buffer beam and was materially reduced by fitting a stronger springing arrangement between engine and tender.

The names given to the engines constituted a delightfully mixed bag, and so reminiscent of the old London & North Western practice that they are well worth recording. The engines were numbered 70000 to 70054, and their names in order (except for No. 70047, which never had a name) were: *Britannia*, *Lord Hurcomb*, *Geoffrey Chaucer*, *John Bunyan*, *William Shakespeare*, *John Milton*, *Robert Burns*, *Coeur-de-Lion*, *Black Prince*, *Alfred the Great*, *Owen Glendower*, *Hotspur*, *John of Gaunt*, *Oliver Cromwell*, *Iron Duke*, *Appollo*, *Ariel*, *Arrow*, *Flying Dutchman*, *Lightning*, *Mercury*, *Morning Star*, *Tornado*, *Venus*, *Vulcan*, *Western Star*, *Polar Star*, *Rising Star*, *Royal Star*, *Shooting Star*, *William Wordsworth*, *Byron*, *Tennyson*, *Charles Dickens*, *Thomas Hardy*, *Rudyard Kipling*, *Boadicea*, *Hereward the Wake*, *Robin Hood*, *Sir Christopher Wren*, *Clive of India*, *Sir John Moore*, *Lord Roberts*, *Lord Kitchener*, *Earl Haig*, *Lord Rowallan*, *Anzac*, *The Territorial Army* 1908–1958, *Solway Firth*, *Firth of Clyde*, *Firth of Forth*, *Firth of Tay*, *Moray Firth*, and *Dornoch Firth*. Many of these names had been carried by engines of the past. One of John Ramsbottom's LNWR Newton class 2–4–0s had been named *Britannia*, and there had been Joseph Beattie's famous 6 feet 6 inches 2–4–0 *Britannia* on the LSWR. An LNWR Prince class 4–6–0 had been *Robert Burns*, and the names *Black Prince* and *Alfred the Great* had been carried by engines of the two different classes of Webb's LNWR four-cylinder compound 4–4–0s. Both an LNWR Crewe Goods of 1850 and Samson 2–4–0 of 1863 had been named *John of Gaunt*. The names *Iron Duke*, *Lightning*, and *Tornado*, had been borne by the famous Great Western Broad Gauge 8-feet singles—engines which for many people were the Broad Gauge—and the 'Flying Dutchman' was the almost legendary train which they hauled. In addition three LNWR engines had been called *Lightning*, a 'single' of 1849, a Newton 2–4–0, and an Experiment 4–6–0. The Star names had belonged to early Great Western Stephenson singles and also Churchward's four-cylinder 4–6–0s. *Charles Dickens* had been one of the most famous of LNWR Precedents, and one of the classic Georges of the same line had been given the same name. *Boadicea* had been commemorated by an LNW Precursor 2–4–0 of 1874 and also by a Webb four-cylinder compound 4–4–0. One of the Great Western Broad Gauge 4–4–0s had been named *Robin Hood* and *Firefly* 'singles' of the same railway had been named *Arrow*, and *Venus*. A Great Central Railway four-cylinder 4–6–0 had been honoured with the name of *Earl Haig*; and so one could go on with this roll of locomotive history. But again in the London & North Western naming tradition, many of the names were quite new.

No. 70004 *William Shakespeare* gained some fame. The engine was given a special exhibition finish for the Festival of Britain in 1952 and for some months was on display on the South Bank site. Later *William Shakespeare* worked the 'Golden Arrow' between Victoria and Dover and became a familiar sight to travellers and station-frequenters with its immaculate livery and gleaming golden arrow on the smokebox door.

On May 25, 1951, *Engineering* said that 'The most rationally minded railway officer, straight from reading the report on electrification, may be forgiven if, as he stands beside *John Milton* on the test bed, he rejoices that the country's economy at the present time will not allow heavy capital expenditure on the electrification of railways'. On the same date the *Railway Gazette*, reporting a test run, said that 'From the times and speed achieved, it would have been difficult for an expert travelling in the train, to have deduced that he was being hauled not by a 105-ton Class 8 4-cylinder Pacific with a tractive effort of 40,300 lbs., but by a considerably smaller 94-ton 2-cylinder engine with a tractive effort of only 32,160 lbs.

Another notable engine was No. 70014 *Iron Duke*, which was first employed on Southern Region Continental boat expresses but was later transferred to the London Midland Region and ran on the old North Western and Midland main lines. On the latter this engine and No. 70032 *Tennyson* were timed at 99 mph on down expresses at the foot of the 5½-mile gradient at 1 in 202 at Flitwick. Mr Cecil J. Allen (in his *British Pacific Locomotives*) believes that the fastest run ever recorded over the lines of the old Great Eastern Railway was made by No. 70035 *Rudyard Kipling*, which covered the 46¼ miles from Ipswich to Norwich in 39 minutes, with a maximum for a full mile past Diss of 94 mph with 325 tons behind the tender.

The record in punctual running of the two-hour 'Broadsman' express, in a service at hourly intervals, was a tribute both to the Britannias and to the enthusiastic crews who handled them. The average consumption of coal and water showed the skill with which the engines were driven on this exacting schedule; but the figures also supported Riddles' contention that theoretical improvement in thermal efficiency may be quite meaningless, because different practices in driving and firing will lead to widely different results with the same engine. Of the average rates of consumption per journey by the Britannias with nine different crews, the lowest was 2,448 gallons of water and 3,060 lbs. of coal, and the highest 3,077 gallons of water and 3,846 lbs. of coal. The intermediate figures were spread fairly evenly between these.

The Class 6 Pacifics, or Clans, were similar to the Britannias, but with a smaller boiler and cylinders. Ten of them were built and all were posted to Scotland. Their running in England was confined mainly to Glasgow trains to and from Liverpool and Manchester. They showed themselves capable of very good performances and were popular with the Scottish engine crews and, indeed, with the Motive Power Department. They had no difficulty in meeting all that was required of them by the time-table. But a disadvantage was their comparatively low adhesive weight of 56 tons 18 cwt. as compared with the 60 tons of the LMS Jubilee 4–6–0s in the same power class. This explains Riddles' regret that he had not built the Clans as 4–8–0s, because if he had the adhesive weight would have been in the neighbourhood of 72 tons, and such an engine should have met all the traffic requirements of the difficult Scottish main lines.

The ten Class 6s were numbered 72000 to 72009 and their names in order were *Clan Buchanan*, *Clan Cameron*, *Clan Campbell*, *Clan Fraser*, *Clan MacDonald*, *Clan MacGregor*, *Clan MacKenzie*, *Clan MacKintosh*, *Clan MacLeod*, and *Clan Stewart*. It had been intended to build another fifteen, ten more for Scotland and five for Southern Region, but it was then decided not to produce any more until experience showed whether the superiority of Class 6 over Class 5 justified the expense of the bigger engine. Dieselization started before a decision had been reached.

The circumstances which led to the construction of a Class 8 Pacific have already been narrated. It had a Britannia boiler barrel and the same sized coupled wheels of 6 feet 2 inches as the Britannias and Clans which Riddles considered large enough for the fastest speeds. It was not practicable to provide two cylinders large enough for the power required, and Riddles chose three rather than four on account of the more even turning moment. A double chimney was fitted to improve the maximum output. Riddles decided on Caprotti poppet valves, which he had always liked and, as recorded in Chapter IV, he had been engaged at Beames's direction in fitting them to some of the Claughtons. Ivatt, too, had tried his adaptation of this gear on the Stanier Class 5s. Riddles had always felt that if the theory of smooth and straight passages for steam was right, then one could hardly improve on a poppet valve, with full exhaust opening at all positions of the reversing gear. Since the mechanical troubles previously experienced had been largely overcome, it was well worth trying, and the manufacturers were most anxious that another trial should be made. Riddles accordingly put proposals to the Executive, which were approved, and instructed the Derby Drawing Office to develop the engine in conjunction with the manufacturers. And so No. 71000 *Duke of Gloucester* was born. It ran freely and well, but did not show up as well as it should have done. Its life was too short for any development to take place, but it was apparent that the boiler proportions were not properly balanced and the front end draughting arrangements needed considerable improvement. There was a lack of powerful exhaust, due no doubt to the exhaust characteristics of the Caprotti gear, and this would have to be corrected. Riddles was satisfied, however, that he had a Class 8 Pacific that was potentially better than any other in the country, and had he remained in his appointment and had steam been given the future that it should have had, he is certain that these troubles, which he might have asked Ell to tackle, would have been cured.

But even allowing for some trouble in steaming, the engine was never given a fair chance. Like Ivatt's prototype diesels, she was the victim of the link system. She required an entirely different driving technique from the LMS Duchesses. A driver might have the new Pacific one day and then LMS types for the next fortnight or more. In any case, all the first Pacifics designed by Churchward, Stanier, Gresley, and Bulleid experienced worse troubles than Riddles' first (and only) Class 8. Indeed, the *Duke of Gloucester* achieved some remarkably good performances, which gave an indication of what might be expected once the draughting trouble had been cured.

If some people expressed doubts about the Class 8 Pacific, none had anything but praise for the Class 9 ten-coupled freight engine. In fact there are strong grounds for regarding it as the most outstanding steam engine ever to run in the British Isles. Detailed design of the engine was undertaken at Brighton, and Riddles says that a great deal of the credit for this is due to R. G. Jarvis, the Chief Draughtsman there.

Soon after the 2–10–0s went into service it was found that they could run freely at very high speeds. They began to appear on passenger trains in various parts of the country, and there were well-documented reports of their exceeding 90 mph. This was a speed within reach of only a comparatively limited number of express locomotive classes. The Western Region (of all administrations!) tried out one of the 2–10–0s in 1960 on the 'Red Dragon' and 'Capitals United' expresses from Cardiff to Paddington and back, turns which the engine apparently handled with ease. (It should be added that this was No. 92220 *Evening Star*, the last engine to be built for British Railways, that she was constructed at Swindon, and that she had Great Western green livery and a copper-capped chimney—so that she was perhaps naturalized into respectability!)

Baron Gérard Vuillet, that most notable French observer of locomotive performance, records in his book *Railway Reminiscences of Three Continents* that he rode on the footplate of No. 92000 (the first of the class and fitted with a double exhaust) hauling the 'Pines Express', loaded to twelve coaches of 458 tons gross. Baron Vuillet recorded the journey over the whole of this formidable route from Bath to Bournemouth West on this engine 'designed for the British Railway by Mr Riddles' and says that it 'was a remarkable effort indeed for an 88-ton locomotive' and adds that the 'run was a magnificent example of skilled driving and firing, with high sustained power and remarkable outbursts of exceptional power, showing the flexibility of the steam locomotive'.

Two notable variations were tried on this class. Ten completed in 1955 were fitted with Crosti boilers. The object of this device was to save heat which would otherwise be wasted. Below the boiler proper was apparently another boiler, but actually a drum which was a pre-heater for feed water. The hot gases from the boiler were turned down into this drum, passed back through it to heat the feed water, and then exhausted through a multiple blast pipe into a flat chimney on the side of the rear end of the boiler. The chimney in the normal position was only used for lighting up and was normally closed. In practice the Crosti boiler showed little saving over the conventional pattern. In Italy good results were obtained on old engines, not on an engine of such efficient modern design as the British 2–10–0. Any slight saving on the British engine was more than counterbalanced by the corrosion of the smokebox and chimney, and in a cross wind the view from the cab was obscured by smoke from the rear-mounted chimney. All ten engines eventually had the Crosti arrangement removed.

In 1959 No. 92250 was fitted with a Giesl ejector, the invention of Dr Adolf Giesl-Gieslingen, an Austrian locomotive engineer. This consisted of an oblong but narrow chimney with seven multiple nozzles in line from front to rear. On older locomotives the Giesl ejector had produced remarkable results, but again, on the very efficient 2–10–0, the improvement was only marginal and the invention was not taken up.

As stated above, most engines were fitted with a single blast pipe and chimney, but, for comparison and with particular reference to maximum output, some were given double blast pipes and chimneys. Apart from the *Duke of Gloucester*, these comprised 80 of the 2–10–0s, the Southern Region quota of Class 4 4–6–0s, and some of the same class allocated to the Western Region. Caprotti valve gear was fitted to thirty of the Class 5 4–6–0s, and Riddles' faith in it was justified by the running of these engines in Scotland and their popularity with their drivers.

With or without Caprotti valve gear, however, the Class 5s were very capable and fast engines, and at times surprised such an expert observer as Cecil J. Allen, with his long experience of timing the Stanier engines of the same power class. The remaining Standard engines did not often come into the limelight, but their performance justified expectations, and Riddles could feel with some satisfaction that he had a stud of engines that could meet all British Railways' traffic requirements for some time to come.

One of the essentials to make the introduction of standard types workable, was a body of men who felt that they belonged to one organization and who were not wedded to the traditions of a former company, regarding any British Railways' product as a foreign intrusion. In order to get this spirit, to use an army terminology, of belonging to a regiment (i.e. region) of one Corps (i.e. British Railways), such as Royal Signals, rather than to an individual cavalry or infantry regiment (i.e. old Company), Riddles transferred senior officers as much as possible from one region to another. By this means he hoped that they would learn to understand one another's problems and gradually adopt a common doctrine and a common line of thought. It is not the least valuable of the legacies which he bequeathed to British Railways.

CHAPTER XVII

Back to Crewe

The last function that Riddles undertook as a member of the Railway Executive was to lay the foundation-stone of the new Crewe Locomotive Works Training School. It was a nostalgic occasion, for he was ending his railway career where he had started it forty-four years before. It was a distinguished gathering, and amongst those present were the Rt. Hon. Lord Glyn of Farnborough, a former Director of the LMS; Sir William Wood, formerly President of the LMS and latterly a Member of the British Transport Commission; Sir William Stanier, a former CME of the LMS; and H. G. Ivatt, the last CME of the LMS. The evening before the ceremony Riddles had presided at the Golden Jubilee dinner of the famous Past and Present Pupils and Premiums of Crewe, and only the second occasion on which this dinner had been held at Crewe. It was a fitting culmination of a great railway career, for the inscription on the stone that he was to lay was inscribed: 'This foundation stone was laid by R. A. Riddles CBE, Member of the Railway Executive, who was himself an Apprentice in Crewe Works, 1909–1913.'

The Training School scheme originated in a conversation between Stanier and Sir Harold Hartley in 1940, as a result of which the former instructed E. J. Larkin (at that time Assistant Works Superintendent, Derby) to go into the matter. Larkin submitted a report early in 1941 and the LMS sent a copy of it to the Board of Education. Larkin's proposals envisaged the establishment of a Works Training School in each of the main Works of the LMS. These would cover all workshop trades, the instructional staff being provided by the LMS. In addition he suggested that the Board of Education should authorize lecturers employed by the local Education Authorities to visit the schools to teach some of the other subjects. The President of the Board of Education was impressed by this report and undertook to support its recommendations.

Authority was given for the establishment of a prototype of these Training Schools at Derby; but owing to the War this was not ready until December 1947, when it was opened by Sir Robert Burrows, Chairman of the LMS. It was agreed that similar schools at the other main LMS Works would be considered if the Derby scheme was successful. This, of course, was right at the end of the existence of the LMS as a separate Company, and though after nationalization it was still possible to say 'London Midland and Scottish' in reference to two regions it did not indicate any post-nationalization imperialism which could implement pre-nationalization decisions. Nevertheless, the scheme was of immediate interest to the British Transport Commission, and as early as January 1948 Members of the Commission and the Labour and Establishment Members of the various Executives visited Derby to see how the scheme was working. It was such an obvious success that they recommended that it should be developed and extended to the larger Works, not only of the London Midland Region, but of all the Executives, as far as possible. This reflected great credit on Larkin, who, in 1953, was Acting Assistant Mechanical and Electrical Engineer London Midland Region. It was he, too, who conceived and planned the Crewe Training School when the authority for it was given in July 1951.

At this new school at Crewe, apprentices were to be trained from the date of their engagement at the age of 15 for a year, the course being divided into three terms. During the year there would be three intakes, one for each of the three terms, the starting dates of which would conform to the leaving dates of schools in the Crewe area. The intake for each term would be 100 boys, making 300 for the year. Of these, 210 would be locomotive works trade Apprentices and 90 for the other technical departments (civil engineer, motive power, and signal and telecommunications). Of the training time about two-thirds was to be spent on practical work (coremaking, fitting and assembly, joinery, electrical, machining, moulding, patternmaking, plating, foundry and smithy, model making, and sheet metal and coppersmith work) and the remaining one-third was divided between workshop mathematics, workshops science, sketching and drawing, individual expression, topical talk, workshop theory, physical education, industrial geography, industrial history, and first aid.

The practical training was intended to provide for each of the following skilled trades employed in the Crewe Works: brass finisher, coppersmith, coremaker, die sinker, electrician, fitter, instrument maker, joiner, moulder, painter, pattern maker, plater, plumber, riveter, sheet metal worker, smith, and turner.

After leaving the school, Trade Apprentices became subject to the progressive system of workshop training, which had first been introduced in Crewe Works in 1943. Trade Apprentices became skilled craftsmen at the age of twenty-one. Some of them were selected for promotion to Engineering Apprentices, and to this class also were recruited boys from public and grammar schools, who received a full engineering training, and pupils, who had to have an engineering degree before being accepted and who spent time in all the main shops.

In the locomotive world, training at Crewe was something of a mystique. There were, it is true, other Works where one could be trained as a locomotive engineer, just as (if rumour is to be believed) there are other methods of becoming an army officer than by qualifying at Sandhurst. Indeed, the list of eminent CMEs who were proud to call themselves 'Crewe men' is a formidable one. And amongst them was this last steam locomotive engineer of all, about to found a school for boys who would never know steam, except as the apprentices to the modern merchant navy learn of the sailing clippers racing home through the great blue rollers of the Indian Ocean and the steep white-capped green seas of the North Atlantic. Yet, at the time of this ceremony, Crewe was still a steam centre. Over 7,000 steam engines had been built there since its foundation. The first of all had been a little 2–2–2 engine of the Grand Junction Railway with 6 feet driving wheels, No. 49 *Columbine* built in 1845, which is still preserved in the Railway Museum at York. The thousandth locomotive was No. 613, turned out in December 1866; one of John Ramsbottom's 'DX' Class 0–6–0 goods engines, of which no less than 943 were built, more than any other British engine and eight more than Riddles' own Austerity 2–8–0s. No. 2000 in the Crewe list appeared in May 1876; a 2–4–0 passenger tank engine designed by Webb, which was properly numbered 2233 but which was photographed as No. 2000. No. 3000 came in July 1887; one of Webb's four compound tank engines, a 2–2–2–2 No. 600. No. 4000 was another Webb compound built in March 1900; a four cylinder 4–4–0 engine No. 1926 *La France*. The five thousandth engine was one of the London & North Western classics, No. 1800 *Coronation*, a super-heated 4–4–0 express passenger engine by C. J. Bowen-Cooke, and built in King George V's Coronation year of 1911. When the six thousandth engine was built the London & North Western had ceased to exist, and LMS No. 13178 was a Horwich designed 'Crab' Class mixed traffic 2–6–0, built in 1930. By the time the seven thousandth appeared in September 1950 British Railways was firmly established, though No. 41272 was a 2–6–2 tank engine of LMS design. And in January 1951 Crewe Works had completed Riddles' own first engine for British Railways, No. 70000 *Britannia*.

To look ahead for a moment, on December 15, 1958, the last steam locomotive was turned out from Crewe Works; it was No. 92250, fittingly one of the type which was Riddles' masterpiece, the Class 9 2–10–0s. She was Crewe's 7,331st steam locomotive. There was, at first sight, little in common between the 1st and the 7,331st, between *Columbine* and No. 92250, but both the first and the last Crewe steam engines had two cylinders placed outside; and the reasons for building them so were somewhat similar. Riddles' insistence on 'get-at-ability' has been mentioned more than once. But that remarkable engineer Joseph Locke also had something to say on the matter when he gave evidence before the Gauge Commission appointed by Parliament in 1845 to enquire into the desirability of making provision to secure a uniform railway gauge. In August 1845 the Commission proceeded to take evidence from the rival protagonists of the 'narrow gauge' (4 feet 8½ inches) and the 'broad gauge' (7 feet). Joseph Locke was Engineer of the Grand Junction, London & South Western, St Germain, Paris & Rouen, and other railways. In relation to locomotives, he was asked whether the question of gauge had exercised him much on the Paris & Rouen line. He replied:

'It did not, for this reason; the difficulties I alluded to before, viz. the complexity of the machinery under the boiler had been got rid of; the outside cylinders which were applied on the Grand Junction first had . . . perfectly succeeded, so that on the Paris and Rouen line I had not the difficulty of the old engines, and I adopted the same description of engines on the Paris and Rouen that had succeeded on the Grand Junction, namely engines with outside cylinders without any machinery under the boiler except the eccentrics. . . . I may state that I, myself, have never found, except in the first instance where our engines were complex, any want of space for the proper working of the engines on the present gauge. . . . We have got rid of a great deal of complexity in the machinery itself, and the complexity which remains is on the outside of the engine and not under the boiler. In that way we have obtained what we wanted, space for our machinery without going to the much greater and much more extraordinary expense of increasing the gauge.'

But if only the far-sighted Locke had increased the British *loading* gauge!

The Commission asked Locke, 'With the inside cylinder there is a liability to break the crank?'

'Yes'; he replied, 'the inside cylinder had necessarily a crank-axle, and we had so many breakages of the crank-axle on the Grand Junction line, that it was not only a source of great expense, but of danger, because the crank broke when the train was going and threw the engine off the line; and therefore, to avoid this, which was a matter of great consequence, we adopted the change which I have suggested.'

(Broken crank axles were very prevalent when Riddles was at Crewe. But when, after his return from Horwich in 1923, he introduced the system of initial inspection, not only was Crewe able to prevent breakages, but a method of marking and examination was devised so that cranks with small flaws were given more life, until the flaw had increased to the extent that the crank was unfit for further service. The practice of this system over many years resulted in the saving of a considerable expenditure on solid cranks.)

The crank axle failures, to which Locke referred, occurred mainly on the two sharp curves with which the north-south

GJR main line joined the Liverpool and Manchester at Newton-le-Willows for through running to and from either of those towns. At that time J. Buddicom was Locomotive Superintendent of the GJR and Alexander Allan was Manager of the Company's Works at Liverpool. Allan had previously worked for the firm of G. Forrester & Co. of Liverpool. George Forester appreciated the advantages of horizontal cylinders, but wanted to move the machinery from under the boiler to make it more accessible. His standard engines, of which three were built in 1834 for the Dublin & Kingstown Railway and one for the Liverpool & Manchester Railway, were the first to have outside horizontal cylinders and were 2–4–0s. On such a short wheel-base they swayed laterally on the road, earning for them the nickname of 'Boxers'. From his experience with these, Allan obtained permission to reconstruct three GJR 2–2–2s with straight driving axles and outside cylinders. The success with these engines led to the building of the so-called 'Crewe' type of 2–2–2 passenger and 2–4–0 goods classes. Locke was so impressed with them that, when he was appointed Engineer of the Paris & Rouen Railway, Buddicom at his suggestion was invited in 1842 to come and design their engines. Some of Buddicom's engines for the Paris & Rouen were in service for seventy years on this line and on the Ouest Railway which absorbed it. They were so successful and so rugged and reliable that many were built for the Paris–Orléans and other railways. However, the history of the Crewe type and its spread to and influence on many railways in Great Britain and France is a story in itself which is outside the scope of the present book. The odd thing is that succeeding LNWR locomotive engineers reverted to the inside cylinder engine and, apart from John Ramsbottom's lovely little *Lady of the Lake* Class 2–2–2s, no mainline engines with two outside cylinders were built at Crewe until the advent of the 'Crab' 2–6–0s of the LMS. (But a purist might object that their cylinders were not horizontal, and that two outside horizontal cylinders had to await the arrival of Stanier.)

The ceremony of laying the foundation-stone of the new school took place on September 22, 1953, and Riddles was due to retire the following week, on September 30th. The proceedings were opened under the Chairmanship of J. W. Watkins, Chief Regional

Officer London Midland Region. After his introductory remarks, Watkins called on the Mechanical and Electrical Engineer London Midland Region, J. F. Harrison, to give a brief description of the Training School. He was followed by the Under-Secretary Ministry of Education who expressed the Ministry's appreciation of the scheme and promised all the help needed. The Mayor of Crewe, Councillor H. H. Griffiths, who had spent thirty-seven years in the railway service, spoke next. He thought that Crewe ought to congratulate itself on having the school built but wished it could have been called some other name than 'school', because he could visualize a child leaving school to go to Crewe Works being told that he was going to school and exclaiming, 'Blimey! What, again!' But it was something that had been wanted for a long time; for it had not been in the interest of the boy, or of the railway, to dump him in the nut and bolt shop, where they made nuts and bolts and dreamed about nuts and bolts, and could not get away from nuts and bolts. Now they were going to be given opportunities.

Alderman J. Wesley Emberton, Chairman of the Cheshire County Council, referred to the time when the first train passed through Crewe on July 4, 1837, and when the place consisted only of a few scattered houses. He pointed to the enormous rate of development since those days. 'It is a very great pleasure', he said, 'to see Mr Riddles who 44 years ago was an Apprentice in these Works. That should be an incentive to the young people who are going to come into this School.'

The Chairman then said that he was going to ask Mr Riddles to perform the ceremony, but before he did so he felt that he ought to say a few words about him, words which to a lot of them were a little sad, because when this occasion had been arranged they did not know of his impending departure. He had had a most eminent service in the railway for 44 years and was now retiring at his own wish from this very honourable service. They were all very, very sorry and they would only say to him, 'A life of service well done. We shall remember you. Good Health and good luck to you in the future.' He would now ask Mr J. M. Harrison, the Architect, to come along and hand over to Mr Riddles a very nice mallet and trowel.

After carrying out the ceremony with mallet and trowel, Riddles said that when he lived in Denver Avenue, Crewe, a gentleman who said that he was a writer, came into the house and said, 'You know, we men of letters admire you men of action.' Riddles continued, 'We have had a lot of speeches this afternoon, but I have been the only one to do a job of work.' He said that his foundations were in Crewe and that not more than 200 yards away he had had the first administrative job of his life. Crewe had been noted, not only for the very finest locomotives, but for some of the best engineers which the world had ever produced. With the facilities provided by the school there was no excuse for not continuing the great and successful efforts of the past. But it was not sufficient to have technical education or even Apprentice Schools. Unless they could contact and be with the craftsmen in the Works they would never make good engineers. These craftsmen of Crewe had in the past themselves trained the engineers. They might not be highly technical, but sometimes it was a mistake to be highly technical because, like some scientists, the highly technical men saw so many dangers that they were afraid to do anything. Many a locomotive had been built in the Works before it had ever been designed, and the success of all the very good locomotive engineers had been largely due to the skill of the craftsmen in the Works for which they were responsible.

The Chairman concluded the proceedings by mentioning other eminent people who were present: Lord Glyn, Sir William Stanier, 'who, as I said earlier at lunch, came from that small railway the Great Western to this bigger railway the London Midland and Scottish', Mr Ivatt, and Sir William Wood, late President of the LMS 'a gentleman whom we all revere very much'. He concluded by presenting Riddles with a book on the history of Crewe.

Riddles' departure was due to a change of Government and the arrival of a new adminstration which was entirely opposed to nationalization. They could not 'unscramble the egg', but they were determined to throw it back into the pan and cook it into a different consistency (with the help of a little diesel oil!). As every soldier knows, it is a great mistake to reorganize unless there are very strong reasons indeed; because reorganization unsettles people and leads to inefficiency until the new organization

Above: Broadside view of No. 92000

Below: Class 9 2–10–0 No. 92086 on a freight train
By kind permission of British Railways

Above: Class 9 2–10–0 No. 92105 on an iron-ore train. *Below:* The last journey on the footplate. *By kind permission of British Railways*

has got into its stride. However, the new Government had decided that the Railway Executive must go.

In August 1952 Riddles was informed that though he might continue in British Transport Commission employment for a further year, it would not necessarily be in his existing capacity. However, it was eventually decided that the Railway Executive should continue in office until September 30, 1953, with Riddles occupying the same appointment. But, when on that date the Railway Executive was abolished, Riddles decided to retire. And so for a third time, to his great regret, he had lost the opportunity of finishing the job. And with the job faded the vision which had first come to him in youth, and which he was at last in the un-dreamed of position of being able to plan—a railway in which the natural fuel resources of the country would be used to feed a network of electrified main lines, and which he had hoped to see started as soon as the economic situation allowed. (Some years ahead it was to be some consolation when the seed that had been sown at that cocktail party at Annécy bore fruit in the 50 c/s electrification of the old London & North Western main line.)

Many tributes followed Riddles into retirement. *Modern Transport*, for instance, in its issue of September 19, 1953, said that under his direction the activities of locomotive carriage and wagon works had been coordinated and the best methods introduced, and that he had been responsible for the design of twelve classes of steam locomotives intended to meet all the requirements of British Railways. Of these nine were already in service, the Class 3 2–6–0 would be ready in November, the 2–10–0 by the end of the year, and the large passenger engine which was the prototype of the twelfth of these classes would be turned out early in the spring of 1954. His new coaching stock of all steel construction had lighter underframes than any previous design, whilst being twice as strong.

Riddles' own farewell letters to the Chairmen of his Policy Committees, composed of men from each region expert in the particular subject they were to report on, show what a large number of these there were and, consequently, the great foundation for uniformity and economy which had been established. These Policy Committees were for:

Tools for Locomotive Boiler Maintenance;
Custody and Distribution of Material for Locomotive, Carriage and Wagon Building Programmes;
Standardization of Locomotive Firebricks;
Locomotive Maintenance Standards;
Autogenous Welding and Gas Cutting;
Manufacture of Drop Stampings;
Modernization of Locomotives of Regional Design;
Works and Outdoor Machinery Plant Maintenance;
Annealing and Testing Loose Lifting Tackle;
Power Brakes;
De-icing of Conductor Rails;
Construction and Maintenance of New Standard Steam Locomotives—Design and Relation to Manufacture;
Chief Locomotive Draughtsmen;
Locomotive Testing;
Mechanical Design Standards for Electrical and Diesel-Electric Locomotives;
Wagon Standards;
Wagon Handling Appliances;
Carriage Warming;
Wagon Repairs;
Production of Steel Carriages;
Carriage Standards;
Wheels;
Train Lighting;
Painting of Locomotives;
Cleaning Materials for General Railway Requirements;
Workshop Practice;
Statistics—Electric Vehicles;
Standard Specifications;
Standardization of Electrical Components;
Civil and Electrical Engineers Joint Sub-Committee for the Standardization of Lighting Practice;
Safety Standards;
Electricity Meters;
Road Motor Maintenance;
Repair Shop Accommodation;
Specifications and Designs for Motor Vehicles.

The demise of the Railway Executive and Riddles' own departure were followed swiftly by a reversal of his traction policy. The modernization of British Railways included the replacement of steam by diesel power but did not include any major electrification scheme. The British Transport Commission ordered in 1955–6 174 diesel-electric and diesel-hydraulic locomotives, in small batches of fourteen different types. These were to be used in a series of trials to determine which were the most suitable for development and adoption by British Railways. In 1957, when only a few locomotives in the lower power range had been received from the manufacturers, it was decided that the rapid introduction of a large diesel fleet would enable the British Transport Commission to realize much earlier the economies they expected from the change from steam. Accordingly, the plan to test prototypes was abandoned and orders were placed for a large number of many different types of locomotives, and the slaughter of steam engines was carried out as rapidly as they could be replaced by diesels. But, as the last steam locomotives disappeared from British Railways, many of the diesels which replaced them were accompanying them to the breaker's yard.

Riddles received offers of directorships from many manufacturing firms. He refused them all, as part-time employment held no attraction for him. He did accept a request from the Benguela Railway in Angola to advise on the reorganization of their Workshops. On his arrival at Lobito he was told that a berth had been booked for him on the night train to Lisboa; but he said that he would rather travel by day so that he could see something of the line. He was told that trains only ran at night, but at his special request a railcar was laid on for a trip by day. It was decorated on its side with a picture of a white elephant, and Riddles, with some natural anxiety, enquired the reason. The somewhat illogical explanation was that the animal was so rare!

Riddles' heart was now set on retiring to the West Country, where he had found a very charming William & Mary period farm house. But he was approached by a Director of Stothert and Pitt with a request to join their Board. He immediately refused, but in response to the plea that the firm had helped him during the War and that there was a Board meeting only once a month, he agreed. But within a year the Chairman became ill and Riddles found himself acting for him. He was soon appointed Chairman himself and was immediately engaged in another very active career that took him five times round the world, visiting India, Africa, Australia, New Zealand, America, and Canada. At the age of 75 he felt it would be better for the image of Stothert and Pitt if he gave way to a younger man and sat back for a well-earned rest. 'And here I am', he writes to the author, 'working like a scalded cat scribbling notes for you, Hugh!'

Some little time after he had retired from British Railways, Riddles arrived at Euston to ride north on the footplate of the *Duke of Gloucester*. It was, he says, a nostalgic day, his last association with steam and the railway: a trip to Crewe with a stop at Rugby. There was an Inspector whom he knew, but the driver and fireman were strangers to him. The driver was unaccustomed to the engine and, though they ran fairly well, they dropped time steadily and arrived at Rugby six minutes late. Whilst in the station, the Inspector turned to Riddles and said, 'Would you like the corner, Sir?' The driver did not know Riddles and looked a little concerned, but the Inspector assured him that he had no need to worry.

Riddles took over the regulator for the last time in his life for the run to Crewe. He says, 'And so we started with me at the throttle. I loved the feel of the engine and the power that I was controlling; and as we picked up speed the engine sang to me'. Under his expert handling the lost minutes were gradually regained; and the *Duke of Gloucester* was racing along the track over which he had ridden on the footplates of so many engines—with clear signals, over the well-known gradients, and observing the familiar speed restrictions. All too soon he was slowing his great engine round the curve into Crewe station; and his mind went back to the days, so many years ago, when as a youth he had watched train after train come into view round this same curve, dead on time after leaving Euston so many hours before; and he wondered whether any steam man could wish for a finer finish. The engine rolled to a stop at just the right place and right on time; for he had picked up all the six minutes that had been lost, and the hands of Crewe station clock signalled mute approval, as they had done for generations of Precursors, Experiments, Georges, Princes, Claughtons, Royal Scots, Princesses, Coronations, Duchesses, and Britannias during the years that a Crewe Apprentice had risen to the greatest pinnacle of steam locomotive engineering in British railway history. And so Robin Riddles passed from the railway service.

BIBLIOGRAPHY

The following have been consulted in the preparation of this book:

AHRONS, E. L., *The British Steam Locomotive 1825–1925*, Ian Allen, London, 1963.

ALLEN, CECIL J., *The Great Eastern Railway*, Ian Allen, London.

ALLEN, CECIL J., *British Pacific Locomotives*, Ian Allen, London, 1963.

ALLEN, CECIL J., *The London & North Eastern Railway*, Ian Allen, London.

BRITISH RAILWAYS, *Crewe Locomotive Works Training School.*

BRITISH RAILWAYS, *Inaugural Run of Main Line Diesel Locomotives on the 'Royal Scot'.*

BROWN, F. A. S., *Nigel Gresley: Locomotive Engineer*, Ian Allen, London, 1962.

BULLEID, H. A. V., *The Master Builders of Steam*, Ian Allen, London, 1963.

BULLEID, H. A. V., *The Aspinall Era.*

CHALLONER, W. H., *The Social and Economic Development of Crewe 1780–1923.*

COOPER, B. K., *Electric Trains and Locomotives.*

COX, E. S., *Locomotive Panorama*, 2 vols., Ian Allen, London, 1965.

COX, E. S., *British Railways Standard Steam Locomotives*, Ian Allen, London, 1966.

CREWE WORKS, *London & North Western Railway.*

DOW, GEORGE, *Great Central*, Ian Allen, London, 1959.

HAMILTON-ELLIS, C., *The Midland Railway*, Ian Allen, London.

HAUT, F. J. G., *The Early History of the Electric Locomotive*, published by the author, Purley, 1952.

HEAD, SIR F. B., *Stokers and Pokers*, Frank Cass & Co, London, 1968.

HOLCROFT, H., *Locomotive Adventure*, Ian Allen, London, 1962.

INSTITUTION OF LOCOMOTIVE ENGINEERS, *Proceedings.*

JENKINSON, D. and ESSERY, R. J., *Locomotive Liveries of the LMS.*

LEWIS, SEAN DAY, *Bulleid: Last Giant of Steam,* George Allen & Unwin, London, 1964.

LIVESEY, H. F. F., *The Locomotives of the LNWR,* Railway Publishing Company, London, 1948.

MACDERMOT, E. T., *History of the Great Western Railway,* revised by Clinker, Ian Allen, London, 1964.

MAIS, S. P. B., *The Royal Scot.*

MASKELYNE, J. N., *Locomotives I Have Known,* Model Aeronautical Press, Hemel Hempstead.

MASON, ERIC, *The Lancashire & Yorkshire Railway in the Twentieth Century,* Ian Allen, London, 1961.

MORGAN, DAVID P., *Diesels West,* Scientific Subscription Service, 1963.

HOCK, O. S., *The Locomotives of Sir Nigel Gresley,* Longmans, London, 1945.

NOCK, O. S., *The Premier Line: The Story of L & NW Locomotives,* Ian Allen, London, 1952.

NOCK, O. S., *Steam Locomotive,* George Allen & Unwin, London, 1957.

NOCK, O. S., *The London & North Western Railway,* Ian Allen, London, 1960.

NOCK, O. S., *Sir William Stanier: A Biography,* Ian Allen, London, 1964.

NOCK, O. S., *History of the Great Western Railway,* Vol. III, Ian Allen, London, 1964.

NOCK, O. S., *The LNWR Precursor Family,* David & Charles, Newton Abbot, 1966.

NORTH BRITISH LOCOMOTIVE COMPANY, *A History of the NBLC.*

POULTENEY, EDWARD CECIL, *British Express Locomotive Development, 1896–1948,* George Allen & Unwin, London, 1952.

POSTAN, M. M., *British War Production*, United Kingdom Civil Series, London, 1952.

'RIVINGTON', *My Life with Locomotives*, Ian Allen, London, 1962.

SAUVAGE, ÉDOUARD ET CHAPELON, ANDRÉ, *La Machine Locomotive*.

SIDNEY, SAMUEL, *The Gauge Commission*, London, 1846.

STEEL, WILFRED L., *The History of the London & North Western Railway*, 'The Railway & Travel Monthly', London, 1914.

TUPLIN, W. A., *North Western Steam*, George Allen & Unwin, London, 1965.

VILAIN, LUCIEN MAURICE, *Un Siècle de Material et Traction sur le Réseau d'Orléans*, Paris, 1962.

VUILLET, BARON GERARD, *Railway Reminiscences of Three Continents*, Nelson, London, 1968.

WALLIS, P. RANSOME, (Editor), *Encyclopaedia of World Railway Locomotives*, Hutchinson, London.

WEIL, PIERRE, *Les Chemins de Fer*.

WILLIAMSON, J. W., *A British Railway Behind the Scenes*, Ernest Benn, London, 1933.

PERIODICALS

The Locomotive, Carriage & Wagon Review, 'Railway Centenary 1825–1925.

The Railway Engineer, 'Reorganization of Crewe Locomotive Works'.

The Railway Executive, 'Mechanical and Electrical Engineering on British Railways'.

The Railway Gazette, 'The Railways of Switzerland'.

The Railway Gazette.

The Railway Magazine.

Various newspapers, documents, reports, papers and correspondence.

INDEX